INSPIRATION

DEFICIT DISORDER

ALSO BY
JONATHAN H. ELLERBY, Ph.D.

RETURN TO THE SACRED:
Pathways to Spiritual Awakening*

WORKING WITH INDIGENOUS ELDERS

YOUR SPIRITUAL PERSONALITY:
Finding the Path That's Right for You (CD)

◉ ◉ ◉

*Available from Hay House

Please visit:

Hay House USA: **www.hayhouse.com**®
Hay House Australia: **www.hayhouse.com.au**
Hay House UK: **www.hayhouse.co.uk**
Hay House South Africa: **www.hayhouse.co.za**
Hay House India: **www.hayhouse.co.in**

INSPIRATION

DEFICIT DISORDER

The No-Pill Prescription to End
High Stress, Low Energy,
and Bad Habits

Jonathan H. Ellerby, Ph.D.

HAY HOUSE, INC.
Carlsbad, California • New York City
London • Sydney • Johannesburg
Vancouver • Hong Kong • New Delhi

Published and distributed in the United States by: Hay House, Inc.:
www.hayhouse.com • *Published and distributed in Australia by:*
Hay House Australia Pty. Ltd.: www.hayhouse.com.au • *Published
and distributed in the United Kingdom by:* Hay House UK, Ltd.: www
.hayhouse.co.uk • *Published and distributed in the Republic of South
Africa by:* Hay House SA (Pty), Ltd.: www.hayhouse.co.za • *Distributed
in Canada by:* Raincoast: www.raincoast.com • *Published in India by:*
Hay House Publishers India: www.hayhouse.co.in

Editorial supervision: Jill Kramer • *Project editor:* Lisa Mitchell
Design: Nick C. Welch • *Interior illustrations:* Nick C. Welch

Library of Congress Cataloging-in-Publication Data

Ellerby, Jonathan H.
  Inspiration deficit disorder : the no-pill prescription to end high
stress, low energy, and bad habits / Jonathan H. Ellerby.
      p. cm.
  ISBN 978-1-4019-2732-5 (tradepaper : alk. paper)   1.   Self-help
techniques. 2. Inspiration. I. Title.
  BF632.E47 2010
  158.1--dc22

                                           2010000172

Tradepaper ISBN: 978-1-4019-2732-5
Digital ISBN: 978-1-4019-2863-6

13 12 11 10   4 3 2 1
1st edition, August 2010

Printed in the United States of America

To my magical wife, Monica,
with endless love for all you have taught me.
And to my magnificent son, Narayan.
I will forever be inspired by you.

CONTENTS

"It matters not how strait the gate,
How charged with punishments the scroll.
I am the master of my fate:
I am the captain of my soul."

— WILLIAM ERNEST HENLEY

⊙ ⊙ ⊙

"This above all: to thine own self be true,
And it must follow, as the night the day,
Thou canst not then be false to any man."

— WILLIAM SHAKESPEARE

INTRODUCTION

The Best and Worst Thing
My Father Ever Taught Me

My father retired when he was about 65 years old. It wasn't really because he wanted to or had to, but it seemed like a good move at the time. A pharmacist turned businessman, he established an extraordinary business in our hometown in Winnipeg, Canada.

"Ellerby and Hall" was a true pharmacy: prescription drugs only. Located near some of the city's bigger hospitals and clinics, it was known for its exceptional customer service, home delivery, and trustworthy relationships with many of the city's physicians. My dad was the sole owner for the majority of the business's history, and he built it from a small start-up to a thriving local fixture.

Over the years, people asked him to sell his business to them, to franchise it, or to add additional locations in town. He was a shrewd businessman and was as cautious as he was ambitious—maybe more cautious. My dad didn't believe in credit or risk. He believed in sound investments, personal integrity, and a conservative approach to life. The pharmacy was successful enough to provide well for our family, and my father had no desire to earn more than what we needed. In addition, the day-to-day dealings were—aside from our family—the center of his life. He didn't want to be divided between numerous locations and multiple staffs and managers. Ellerby and Hall was his child, his pride, and in many ways, his identity. Beyond love of family, most people would say that it was his life.

But times change and so do industries. Eventually, there was less room for a prescription-only pharmacy that had so much less to offer than a convenience store that stocked everything from chewing gum to lightbulbs and diapers. So when a large Canadian chain of "drugstores" offered to buy his store as well as his inventory, he knew that as difficult as it was, at age 65, it was time to let it go.

After the retirement parties and transition/consulting phase had passed, everyone wondered what my dad would do next. He was smart, well traveled, and had a solid financial nest egg beneath him. My mom was, and still is, an energetic and open-minded woman. Truly, the sky was the limit for them. Dad, however, had lived his dream and really wasn't receptive to new ideas or adventures. His practical and conservative nature served a fine purpose in business, but it impaired many of his relationships—most of all, his relationship to himself. He had few personal pleasures or pastimes, and just a few close friends.

I always thought that there were so many things he could have gotten involved in, but his first year of retirement passed quickly, and he had spent most of it doing little more than walking the dog, reading the newspaper, and turning simple daily errands into time-consuming expeditions. He also began to take regular naps that seemed to get longer as the year passed. Of course, there was more to how he spent his time than that, but the simplicity and lack of direction was a bit of a shock coming from a man who had always been busy, rarely resting, and certainly not lazy. The main concern wasn't that he wasn't "busy," but that he didn't seem to be enjoying himself either. A hobby, a new interest, even some well-deserved indulging would have made sense. He just seemed to drift. He wasn't engaged, even in his resting.

It shouldn't have surprised me that next year when he went to the doctor for a checkup and came home with "asthma." He'd become increasingly tired, and his respiratory health seemed to be declining. Yet I was shocked by the diagnosis. My dad was the kind of man who never got sick. I can scarcely remember a day he missed work. He rarely had a sore throat, cold, or flu. He was just one of those naturally resilient people. If he was sick, I'm sure he simply hid it well and continued on with life. Far from a health nut, one thing my dad was for sure was *robust*. I guess that's why having asthma seemed so odd. Such a late development in life, such a manageable condition, and yet it seemed to be hitting him so hard.

Later that year, we learned that the doctor and his tests were wrong after all. By the time we realized they'd made a mistake, the newly discovered cancer in his lungs had spread widely and was already in his brain. Nine months later, he died.

Did my dad die of cancer? Yes. Did he suffer because of a doctor's mistake? Yes. Was it genetic, or did his lifestyle have an impact? I'm sure both played a part. But I think that all these things were just symptoms of what really killed him: *an inspiration deficit.*

It was hard for anyone to put it into words, but most of us felt the same way: when he gave up his business, it was like he gave up everything. His store was his life and his identity—it was the one piece of him that was truly his own. He loved my brother, sister, and me dearly, but we all had each other and he shared us with our mom. He had Mom, of course, but she had us and her own friends and interests as well. My father knew that she wanted a new life with him; she was ready for major change and a new direction. Retirement could have been a gift, but he didn't see things that way. New horizons weren't appealing to my dad, and change was even less appealing. His business was the one thing that he created, fed, and identified with throughout his adult life. And when he let it go, he lost himself—and that is not a metaphor.

Sadly, my father taught me the most important lesson of my life, and it cost him his own. He showed me that even the things that were once our passions can, in time, become old roles that keep us stuck and from growing. He showed me the risk of allowing life to become too narrowly defined, and identity too singular in nature. We must also remain whole people, complex, evolving, and inspired.

My dad's death showed me that inspiration is a state of being; it's not what you do or have. Passion is a state of mind; and it can flow from one role to the next, one stage to the next, and one relationship to the next. Inspiration is about your inner world, and it is certainly not about doing what you have always done. If you attach your inspiration or identity to anything outside yourself, you stand to become a strange kind of victim in your own design, dependent on the world around you to sustain you and validate you. The inspiration that was my dad's business became a habit and jaded story. Worse than the fact that the inspiration that was once his business had turned into his identity was the fact that he had no other sources of vitality and joy. In that absence, life lost its power.

My dad didn't have the capacity to see what he had to live for. He didn't have the tools or mind-set to look for the opportunities in front of him, nor did he know how to ask for help. In part, it was his generation and culture. It was also his personality and emotional history that kept him trapped in what was safe, unable to imagine that anything new or unfamiliar could be better or even as good as what he knew.

My father was a very intelligent man, almost a genius in some respects. In many ways, he had all a person could want. I loved and admired him deeply, yet I also knew that his inability to truly connect with his heart and allow himself to tap into his own joy and self-awareness choked the vitality out of his life. He paid the price of his inner disconnect on a daily basis, as well as in many of his relationships. In the end, I believe, his inspiration deficit took his life.

Who Is This Book For?

> *"Healing may not be so much about getting better, as about letting go of everything that isn't you—all of the expectations, all of the beliefs—and becoming who you are."*
>
> — RACHEL NAOMI REMEN, M.D.

The first question that most people might ask themselves when they pick up this book is: *Is this for me?* The most straightforward answer is *yes.*

Why? Because this book is about *you*. It's about your greatest chance for health, happiness, and success; and your greatest tendencies to get stuck, develop bad habits, and make poor choices. It's about a most perplexing universal human condition: *Inspiration Deficit Disorder*. And it's about the most promising universal human opportunity: a joyful, vital, and inspired life.

Based on my experience, I believe that Inspiration Deficit Disorder is at the heart of what troubles and challenges most people today. The heart of this book is a road map for improving, healing, or transforming just about any aspect of life you can imagine. I've applied the principles of this approach while working with thousands of people; and I've presented my techniques hundreds of times to therapists, medical doctors, psychologists, celebrities, Fortune 500 executives, nurses, moms, dads, high-school students, addicts, religious leaders, yoga teachers, meditators, retirees, spiritual seekers, and more. The feedback is almost always the same: it's simple, it's clear, and it works.

The basic elements of my teachings aren't new; they're timeless and found in cultures and healing systems around the world. It is the presentation that is new: clear-cut and easy to apply. This book will empower you to take what you already know about yourself and use it to revitalize your life. Everything you know about motivation, healing, psychology, success, and personal betterment will fit into a map that will allow you to see your life and potential more clearly.

It doesn't matter what you do, who you are, or how old you are. Just like the moon and the stars, the seasons, and the cycles of birth and death, your life unfolds within the laws of nature—*human nature*. If you understand the natural laws of self and health, you can quickly learn to tap into the wisdom and energy already acting on you and within you every day.

How to Use This Book

This book is designed to give you the awareness to understand yourself and others in a way that will empower you to experience change. *This is a handbook for the human journey. It presents a simple way to understand the essential elements of life: stress, habits, health, energy, addiction, sex, communication, aspiration, expectation, manifestation, disappointment, emotion, psychology, spirituality, family, service, success, happiness, purpose, vitality, God, and even enlightenment.*

This may sound like a big promise, but the truth is that you already possess all the wisdom you need. The following chapters don't just give answers; they provide you with a method to help you remember the answers that you already carry deep within. You'll be able to get out of your own way and enjoy the magnificent life you were born to experience. The root of what keeps the majority of us from fulfilling this potential is what I call *Inspiration Deficit Disorder.*

Is Inspiration Deficit Disorder a Real Medical or Psychological Term?

Inspiration Deficit Disorder sounds a bit funny, right? It seems clinical but comical. No, it isn't "real." The term is meant to be laughable since it suggests that the very normal process of being human and falling out of balance is somehow a "disorder." That is intentional; it pokes fun at our obsession with labeling people's troubles and challenges and turning everything into a syndrome, disorder, or condition. Inspiration Deficit Disorder is a play off the term *attention deficit disorder*, which gets wildly overused, in my opinion.

It reminds me of a cartoon I once saw of a serious and concerned-looking physician standing before a panicked-looking patient. The patient appears healthy, but sits shocked and afraid on the edge of the examining table. The caption shows the doctor's comment, which was something like: "This may take some time to treat, and I'll need to see you again. You have Symptom Deficit Disorder!" Of course, this means that the problem is that there *is* no problem. The meaning behind Inspiration Deficit Disorder, however, is no joke.

Inspiration Deficit Disorder is about losing your vitality and purpose, and forgetting your original source of love and potential. It's about the cost of being disconnected and unaware of your own unique talents, needs, and destiny. It's about a life of reaction (driven from the outside in) and the difficulties in communicating with others and finding a lasting sense of calm. In one way or another, it's about all of us.

These days people don't often take their stresses, choices, and challenges seriously enough. Instead, they wait until the costs become painful, hopeless, or overwhelming. The symptoms of this pattern of disconnection, although common, aren't really necessary, nor are they the way we were designed to live. That's why I call it a "disorder." My goal is to draw your attention to the fact that you really don't need to have high stress, bad habits, or imbalance in your life. Much of what you've come to accept is *common* but *not* natural in the sense that it isn't optimal or somehow inevitable. Understanding Inspiration Deficit Disorder will change the way you view health and healing, as well as the way you make choices about managing stress and seeking success.

A Joke That Could Save Your Life

Please seriously consider this: *Prolonged and exaggerated experiences of an inspiration deficit can lead to loss of relationships, severe health problems, and mental illness. I have no doubt about this, nor do I make any apologies for this claim. Extreme cases result in symptoms much like addiction, post-traumatic stress disorder, compassion fatigue, and often worse. Inspiration Deficit Disorder can make a bad situation worse, and I believe that it's the source of the high levels of stress that the medical community now widely agrees is the number one cause or aggravator of illness in America. Inspiration Deficit Disorder is serious.*

Some people think that treatment for this disorder should solely be in the hands of medical professionals. On the contrary, it's fundamentally a spiritual condition, which medical doctors and psychologists can heal only certain aspects of. At the heart of the high stress, low energy, and bad habits is a misunderstanding of self, energy, and original creative source. When you heal your awareness of these things, you can energize and heal your life.

In my book *Return to The Sacred: Pathways to Spiritual Awakening,* I document much of my inner journey and share stories of my own moments of healing and spiritual awakening. I consider it a testament to my commitment to explore the extremes of health, healing, and consciousness far beyond the boundaries of "normal." For those who would like more insight into the spiritual tools and sacred world that await us once we move beyond stress and healing, that book may help.

This book, however, concerns everyday living . . . *inspired living*. It's about what I've learned from the clients I've worked with over the years; as well as the things I've personally experienced along the way as a counselor, corporate executive, business consultant, chaplain, spiritual healer, and interfaith minister. Through my Ph.D. in comparative religion, my cross-cultural health research background, and my seminary studies, I've been fortunate enough to travel extensively and study with teachers and healers of diverse cultures and traditions—from leading Western physicians to shamans and sages in the traditional cultures of North America, Africa, and India. Over the course of this journey, I've come to see that Inspiration Deficit Disorder is not only an age-old phenomenon, but also that its remedies are universal and timeless.

I've been honored to witness hundreds (perhaps, thousands) of people actually identify their specific inspiration disorders and end them, without pills or years of expensive therapy. Indeed, people have overcome them with joy, adventure, and self-love. More than anything, these individuals have shown me what works. They are the real experts of transformation, and I'm just a fortunate observer—a support and mirror. My role is to listen carefully and pay attention. I apply what I learn in my own life as a husband, father, son, and citizen; and I try to live what I teach, test it again, and share what valuable information I've gathered as best I can.

A Supplement, a Complement, a Solution—but Not a Replacement

The Inspiration Deficit Disorder identity map (which will be discussed in Part I) and corresponding steps to de-stress, grow, and find meaning and vitality are universally relevant to all people regardless of background or level of education. The approach to working with the system in this book is compatible with whatever your faith or worldview may be. The teachings herein are meant to enhance the tools and philosophies you already believe in—not to replace them. Religion and spirituality (or the absence of these things in your life) are your choice and your own personal matter.

As you'll see, the basic model throughout doesn't require you to desert your culture or join a new one. The path to inspiration begins where you are, with who you are. For many of you, it will unfold seamlessly without any intentional use of the word *spirituality* or even an interest in the subject. By the time you've moved into an inspired life, however, that may change.

At this point, I also want to emphasize that the term *Inspiration Deficit Disorder* and my opinions in no way represent conventional medical or mental-health diagnoses or treatments. *This book is not meant to replace professional help if you feel that you might have a serious condition, situation, or health problem.* In other words, if you're in trouble and fear for your health or safety, get help! You can take this book with you to the waiting room, treatment program, women's shelter, hotel, hospital, spiritual retreat, prison, or wherever your urgency demands you to go.

The End of Inspiration Deficit Disorder

The first step to reclaiming your power and potential is to fully realize where you are right now and how you got there. Knowing this will help you identify the limiting beliefs, emotions, and energies that are actually working against you—even when your intentions are good.

Remember that what you have in your hands is a map to understanding your life experiences up to this moment. It's a way to help you sort out the choices you have before you and the terrain you've become familiar with, as well as the uncharted areas that you may fear, yet long to travel.

The first part of the book will walk you through the process of self-awareness and the formation of Inspiration Deficit Disorder. It will also give you the language and insight that will be necessary for putting the information in Part II to work. The second Part of the book is shorter, but it's focused on solutions and new choices. Its principal theme is action and change. Some of the changes will be easy and fun, and some will be scary and strange—whatever the case, *you* have to do the work.

It's absolutely possible to transform your life beginning today, but you need willingness, honesty, and courage to examine how you think, feel, and act. I can provide a map and point out some good routes, but you must take the journey. Remember that inspired living is a choice.

Be brave, be loving, and begin!

Author's Note: All of the stories and case studies in this book are true; however, all names have been changed to protect the privacy of the individuals involved. In some instances, the stories in this book are composites of similar cases or situations.

◎◎◉◎◎

PART I

A MAP OF YOUR INNER LANDSCAPE: WHO YOU ARE AND WHO YOU AREN'T

*"There are two ways to live your life—
one is as though nothing is a miracle,
the other is as though everything is a miracle."*

— attributed to ALBERT EINSTEIN

Part I Overview: How Did I Get Here?

To understand how to move from where you are to where you want to be, the most critical part of your foundation is awareness. From awareness comes choice. Part I is about helping you understand yourself. You'll be able to see when you're making clear, intentional choices and when you're living out of habit, reaction, or fear. To help you master your life, we'll create a map of your inner landscape that will reveal where your power, potential, and pitfalls lie. This will allow you to see how you arrived at the present moment and what your future

1

may hold. It's essential to know this in order to fully comprehend the big picture of your life. The last thing you want to do is carry the errors and mistakes of the past into the future.

To move ahead with clarity, look for past lessons and expose the roots of the limits you're facing today. Put things in perspective. Regardless of your intention—to just get by, to enhance your own health and healing, to attain success, or to achieve total spiritual awakening—the same principles hold true for all: your best next step will come with a keen sense about how you got where you are.

Before you get started, here's a brief outline of what you can expect in the first nine chapters.

A Map and a New Language

As I've mentioned, the first Part of this book gives you a map to help you determine where you are in your life right now. This same map can be used on an on-going basis to gain perspective and awareness of your specific situations and choices. You'll develop a new and simple language with which you can understand your own history and communicate your present experiences. The language and map are provided in a way that integrates psychological, spiritual, and energetic models of health and healing.

An Evolving Picture

At the heart of Part I is an evolving diagram that will help you visualize all aspects of yourself. Know that how it relates to you will vary based on your stage of life, and even from situation to situation. When you learn to think in terms of this diagram, you'll find yourself looking at life differently.

Living from the Inside Out

The first two chapters introduce you to the basic mind-set that will help you get the most out of the guidance and tools in this book. Almost immediately, you'll start to look at life (and yourself) from a fresh perspective. Fundamental to this first step is the understanding that everything you need in order to effect the greatest change is already within you. You'll see how health, vitality, peace, and a genuine sense of success come from *congruence*—that is, living from the inside out. Living inside out is often called authenticity or integrity; it means that your actions reflect your highest intentions on a daily basis.

The Five Universal Aspects of Self

The rest of Part I introduces the five most fundamental and universal aspects of human nature and experience: **Original Source, Essential Self, Wall of Wounding, Persona**, and **Energy Hooks.** Through understanding these simple layers and dynamics of self, you'll see how (and why) you change, how to develop a sense of mastery over your own changes, and how the world impacts you. Much of this will relate to the forces of old hurts, disappointments, disconnections, and losses and the ways in which they've contributed to the creation of the unconscious masks you wear and the stories you create. The key to freedom from these negative habits, reactions, and addictions lies in identifying the role of energy in your daily life. You'll learn to assess your own energy level (as well as others') to bring clarity and balance to your choices.

◎◎◉◎◎

CHAPTER ONE

The Medicine Is
Already Inside You

*"The secret is alignment: when you know for sure
that you're on course and doing exactly what you're
supposed to be doing, fulfilling your soul's intention,
your heart's desire . . . you are your most powerful."*
— OPRAH WINFREY

A Light on a Dark Night

Alex wasn't what most people would consider to be
a well-educated man, nor was he wealthy in any material way. The work that he used to do day after day was
forgettable by most standards, but Alex was not.

He and I met in a rehabilitation hospital in Winnipeg, Canada, on a cold winter night. At the time, I was
an intern in a spiritual counseling chaplaincy program.
I was making my rounds, moving from room to room,
checking in on the patients of the spinal-cord-injury
wing. I'd stop and chat with the individuals I knew and
invite a connection with those I hadn't yet met. My as-
signment wasn't a religious one; rather, it was simply to
provide counsel and comfort for people in need.

The quiet halls and dark rooms were animated by large windows that revealed the night. The wind was blowing outside, and I noticed the snow dancing in the glow of the streetlights below. There was something captivating about watching a chaotic scene, silent and distant through the thick glass that protected all of us in the hospital. I sighed in relief feeling my good fortune, glad not to be out on such a bitterly cold night. It was a warm feeling of safety and calm. The unit was tranquil; it seemed that no one had much to say. I remember musing that perhaps it was a night for reflection. The storm outside wasn't only affecting me—it had cast a quiet spell over everyone there.

Finally, I approached the last room in the long, wide corridor. A pretty woman, about 30 years old, had just left with two beautiful young girls, maybe ages five and eight. They were dressed simply, and it seemed as though maybe some of their clothes were very old or bought secondhand. A cloud of sadness seemed to hang over them, yet there was a definite sense of strength in their faces. They walked closely together and as they spoke to one another, their tone suggested that they'd shake off the heaviness around them and soon be laughing again.

I knocked on the door and a man's bright voice answered, "Come on in!" A bit surprised, I walked in and glanced around the room. One of the beds was empty, and in the other was a young man about 33 years of age. He had a mustache and shaggy shoulder-length brown hair that was brushed back. He was sitting up in bed, and although the room was sterile and drab, there was something light and vibrant about the space. I introduced myself, and he told me that his name was Alex.

I explained why I was there and let him know that if he needed someone to talk to, I'd be happy to hang out for a while. He asked about the title of my department, saying, "'Spiritual Care,' huh? Is that like religion?" Alex's speech and accent suggested that he had likely grown up in a rural area or perhaps without a great deal of formal education.

"Well," I stammered, unsure of his perspective, "for some, it could be about religion. But spirituality is really more personal. It's about how you answer the big questions in life: what matters, why you are here, which relationships are most important—stuff like that. I try to help people answer those questions."

"Ah, I see. I'm glad you do." His reply surprised me, and I listened as he continued. "I'll tell you what . . . I don't know how I'd make it through this if I didn't know them things. But sure as shit, I'm clear about true things!"

True Things

Alex's confidence and word choice confused me. "What do you mean?" I asked.

"I might not know much, but I know *enough*. My dad made sure of that. He said that in life there are 'true things,' and as long as you know some true things, you can get through anything. I sure learned that the hard way over the years. Now that I'm in a bit of a predicament, I see he was right. The true things always last."

Intrigued, I sat down beside his bed. "Tell me more about 'true things,' Alex."

"Sure. First off, my true things aren't your true things. For me, they've always been the smell of a campfire, the feeling of the soft earth in the spring after the snow melts, the smell of wet hay in the fields, old Chevy trucks, and the music of John Denver and Gordon Lightfoot." He grinned and got a far-off look in his eyes.

"Damn," Alex said softly, as if he'd just had a little taste of his favorite ice cream for the first time in years. "Do you see what I mean? But it's much more than that."

I leaned in to listen.

"A month ago I was in an accident on an icy road. I'd been putting off getting new tires with a better tread for the winter because I wanted to save money. I was working as a plumber's assistant. I did a lot of lifting and carrying—pipes, hoses, tools . . . you get the idea. One night, just like this one, I was driving home from work and hit a patch of ice. My car started to spin out of control, and I skidded right into a lane of oncoming traffic . . . and *bam!* I was hit in the driver's side by a big ol' semitrailer.

"My car was pretty much crushed, and so was I." Alex moved the dinner tray off his lap and patted the outline of two large plaster casts hidden beneath the blankets. "These don't work anymore. My legs were broken in a bunch of places, and my spine was damaged, too. They say I'll never walk again.

"Who could have seen that coming?! Now we're shopping for a handicap van for me and my wheelchair. My brother is building ramps in every part of our house you can imagine so that when I get home, life can go on. And it will . . . because that's a true thing. Life always goes on—you can count on that. You just have to decide if *your* life is going to go on!"

Look for the Lesson

"Aren't you angry? You're a very young man to face something like this," I offered.

"Well, I was at first. Mad at myself and feeling guilty for not fixing my tires. Angry at the ice on the road. Angry at the truck coming my way. But then I realize that I'm glad I didn't crash into a car with a family in it. Others could have been hurt. It could have been worse. I could have been killed. There are a lot of maybes in any situation, but I can only face the true things: I'm here and I'm glad.

"I love my wife and two little girls more than the world. That's a true thing. I'd do anything for them, and the last thing I'd ever want is to leave them without a daddy. My family is the most important thing to me. That's a true thing. I've seen other folks in here. They lose their ability to walk, have sex, or what have you . . . and yeah, it's awful. But you know what's more awful is that they get so sad and angry that they lose everything else, too. They pay so much damn attention to what they lost and who they used to be that they can't see what they have. That's what my dad would call a wasted life. I guess they just don't understand true things."

"You have a smart dad," I added.

"Yes, and I'll make him proud. I know he's watching over me, remindin' me to be grateful. I survived, I still have my family, no one else was hurt, and I still got my hands. I was always good with my hands . . . I'll find something else to do.

"My wife's been telling me that I may have lost my legs, but I haven't lost what makes me who I am. She says it's my 'smarts and hearts' that matter. I think it's just that I make her laugh. Whatever it is, the accident left me with my life, my wits, and my family. So I figure I have everything I need.

"My motto has always been to stick close to the ones I love, try to brighten other people's day, and find a way to get the bills paid on time. The true things about me can't be wrecked in a car crash—they're mine and they're untouchable. That's how I know I'll be fine."

Keep It Simple

I only got to chat with Alex on two more occasions. Soon after we met, he was discharged from the hospital and continued his rehab at home. The head nurse told me that he was in and out faster than anyone she could recall: "He was healing as if the injury wasn't nearly as bad as it was. If I hadn't seen it for myself, I wouldn't have believed it. We'll all miss him. The nurses looked forward to seeing him every day because *he* made *us* feel good. Alex is an angel—a true inspiration."

Two months later, Alex was back in the hospital for an examination and some adjustments to his medications and physiotherapy program. He was already getting around with ease in a wheelchair. I almost cried when he told me that he and his father-in-law had built a set of horizontal wooden bars for him to support himself on to practice walking. He explained that he'd been using them to try to walk even though his doctors told him not to. It created a great commotion for his care team. The amazing conclusion was that the attending physician had begun to consider the possibility that Alex might regain some limited movement and the ability to stand with crutches after all.

I never found out what became of Alex, but I'll never forget the way he inspired me with his spirit and his "true things." I still feel emotional when I think of how courageous and positive he was. Somehow he knew that if he just stayed soul centered, everything else would be okay. I'm sure that it was.

People like Alex prove that health and happiness are an inside job. You can't hang your expectations on external things and be satisfied. An inspired life is not about *what* you do—it's about *how* you do it. An inspired life is about what Alex called "true things." It's about listening to your heart and making choices that honor your essence. The incredible thing is that behind all the expectations you've picked up along the way, you already possess everything you need to make the changes you desire. You came into the world with all the ingredients needed for a vital, balanced life.

Sadly, the world is a busy, distracting, and sometimes hurtful place. Although the ingredients for an inspired life can never be taken from a person, many of us lose the recipe or never put those ingredients to use.

Willingness and Action

Alex's story is absolutely true, and the experience gave me incredible insight into the healing power of trusting the answers you carry within. There are certain laws of change, success, and fulfillment that are universal. You'll learn them (and be reminded of them) throughout this book. No one can give you the most crucial elements, however. Alex had them. Most important, he had the willingness to transform his situation for the best, no matter what it took.

You can know all the philosophies and have all the books and motivational CDs in the world, but if you don't have the willingness to put their teachings into practice —to take some risks and invest some energy—nothing changes and Inspiration Deficit Disorder takes over.

Don't Believe Anything You're Told about Transformation

Beliefs are like bridges. They can be helpful for short periods and can make all the difference in a journey. A belief can carry you across a raging river of change, but in the end, you can't live on one. Your greatest life won't come from simply believing in something. To say "I believe it" is to say "I hope it is true." If you want to understand the ideas and practices in this book, don't believe me, try them for yourself. Then you will *know*. If you doubt something you've read here, try it out. Then you will know. If you want to bring anything into being, live as if it were already real. Then you'll embody the evidence for yourself. If the evidence comes, keep going. If it doesn't, ask a new question, modify your plan, get some advice, and get moving.

A Different Kind of Knowing

During the days of my master's and Ph.D. programs, I did a lot of traveling and spent a great deal of time among indigenous cultures. In fact, many of my best friends, mentors, and extended family at the time were Native American. One of my greatest teachers was a Lakota Sioux healer named Wanagi Wachi (a man whom I refer to quite a bit in my book *Return to The Sacred*). The contrast between the *way* I was learning in university settings and the way I learned from my African and Native American mentors was shocking. In "school" there was a lot of reading, looking up facts, gathering references in journals and books, and in-class discussions and lectures.

However, there were no lectures, books, or references among the traditional communities. Wanagi Wachi would say, "In my culture, our most valued schooling is from the universe-ity, not the university. I won't tell you what to believe. I can share my experiences with you and lead you into your own. Silence, nature, prayer, and listening to your heart will teach you all you need to know. If you don't understand something, don't push it away. Welcome it and try to relate to it. If you are patient, it will reveal itself in time."

What he said was true. During the first seven years of the eleven-year period when I was regularly spending time with him as a student and his spiritual son, he never lectured to me. He never explained the ceremonies or healing practices we were involved in or why. Instead, he helped me learn through experience.

It may be hard for some to believe, but he simply showed me—through meditation, prayer, and self-awareness—that somewhere deep inside my body and soul lived all the answers I needed. Indigenous scholars call this *embodied knowing*. It's the idea that just by trying something, doing something, or interacting with something, understanding follows. In the Western world, we still recognize this concept. In professional terms, it's known as a practicum, an internship, or a trial period. It's a common approach in modern medicine and other therapeutic professions.

You've probably even said something like this to yourself, a friend, or family member: "I can't *tell* you, and you really can't get it from a book. You just have to try it, and then you'll understand." Life is like one of those funny jokes between friends. Later on, as you try to explain it to someone else, you say, "You just had to be there."

From Experience to Knowing

Experience and knowing are at the heart of this book, and I do feel that experience will become the currency of the next age. People are already becoming tired of ideas, theories, and philosophies. Today, we want to be involved, we want to connect. More and more people long to end the disconnection, the lack of touch and firsthand encounters. We've spent enough time looking at screens and listening to experts.

Now is the time to move beyond what you believe and build a life based on what you feel in your heart and what you know in your bones. *Inspiration is not an idea; it is an experience.*

◎◎◉◎◎

CHAPTER TWO

The Beginning of the End

"Once we realize that imperfect understanding is the human condition, there is no shame in being wrong, only in failing to correct our mistakes."

— GEORGE SOROS

Tied Down by a Thread

Have you ever felt the need for change, but were at a loss as to how to go about it? Or perhaps you knew that a change was necessary, but no matter what you tried, you somehow always ended up back where you started. It's as if an invisible force was keeping you in place.

How is it that we all know what we want to do but have such a hard time doing it? What stands between us and our New Year's resolutions and late-night promises? The simplest adjustments or shifts often escape us—sticking to a new plan or diet, communicating better, being kinder (or less angry), or experiencing deeper peace, for example—sometimes seeming impossible.

It reminds me of something I learned while traveling through Asia. It was a little piece of folk wisdom that caught my attention and eventually changed my life.

Buddhist monks, Hindu yogis, Christian missionaries, and fellow travelers all knew this simple axiom; and strangely, it followed me wherever I went. Like a buoyant piece of wood in a rushing stream, it showed up in surprising places, was soon forgotten, and then reappeared. The first time I heard it, I thought it was interesting but not personally meaningful to me in any way I could understand. It was only when I returned home that it hit me.

I was ready for a new life—one that would be full of inspiration, ideas, and connection. *But to my surprise, I found that everything I had hoped to leave behind was still there waiting for me when I got back.* I'd experienced a life-altering adventure, yet within days of my return, all my old habits and reactions were working to undo those changes, rising up and blooming like the irrepressible grass between the cracks in the sidewalk.

Had I traveled the world only to come home and be just as stuck as I was when I left? Had I meditated with Tibetan monks and prayed in mosques and cathedrals only to *still* bite my nails and forget to pay my bills on time? I had been purified in ancient hot springs by a circle of Maori healers and danced in the initiations of an African tribe, but I continued to argue with my mother about the most mundane and absurd things. How is that possible?

That's when I took another important step in unraveling the delicate tangles of my own inner thoughts and feelings and ultimately realized one of the key starting points to the journey of healing, inspiration, and emotional freedom. Suddenly, I remembered that little gem of wisdom I'd heard so many times while abroad, and everything made sense. It all has to do with choice.

It all has to do with power and family. It has to do with
. . . an elephant.

It's said that in Southeast Asia, elephants have been
domesticated for thousands of years as a result of a simple trick. Have you wondered how such a mighty beast
could have been controlled by the puny efforts of humans long before the days of tranquilizer darts, iron
cages, and electrical prods? The answer was surprising.

Training an Elephant

If an elephant can be captured when it's young, the
only thing the trainer needs to do is tie the animal to a
tree just big enough to hold it and with a rope just strong
enough that it can't break. Since the elephant is young,
a simple post or small bush would work, and the rope
could be just a piece of twine or string.

The young animal is easily confused and restrained.
It attempts to escape, but the effort and pain of pulling
free quickly feels intimidating and limiting. The inexpe-
rienced elephant learns that it will never break the cord
or uproot the post. The unrealized giant simply gives up.

In time, the elephant will grow, gaining thousands
of pounds and several feet in height. Eventually, that
small pachyderm will become one of the largest, most
powerful land animals in the world. But here's the trick:
the same rope and tiny tree can still hold the same elephant in place! *Although it is mighty beyond imagination,
it has come to believe in its limits.* The powerful elephant
isn't imprisoned by the restraints, but by itself. Its belief that it cannot be free is what keeps it stuck. It can't
see beyond what it knows. *It holds an outdated personal*

experience as the formula for life. Its life reflects an old lesson: you will never be totally free again.

Of course, this limit isn't real. The elephant is free and able and more powerful than it knows. But those who captured and now interact with the elephant will never allow it to know its true greatness, for fear that they'll be overcome by the animal. They worry that if the elephant knew its full potential, it would break free. Then they'd lose everything they've come to depend upon and expect.

An Old Way of Being

There are many ways to explain this story of how the elephant is tied down by a string. Some call it *self-limiting thoughts, learned helplessness,* or *conditioning.* No matter how you explain the neurology and psychology of it, the lesson is clear. We're all like the trapped elephant in one way or another. Some of us enjoy our traps and even like our trainers or the circus we perform in. In some respects, we're all adhering to limits set long ago— boundaries that we had little or no part in consciously creating or choosing.

You and I are like the great giant that has come to believe in the limits that others have created for it. Your potential to change is extraordinary. Your talent and energy is extreme, but it may be so long since you've touched the raw electricity of your spirit that you forget what it's like. Perhaps the people around you are like those who suppress the elephant. They're afraid of change, terrified that you'll leave them, or worse, that you expect them to change as well. Know that you are capable of far more than you realize in more areas of your life than you could imagine. You'll never really know until you try, though.

Dare to Dream

I'd like you to turn your attention to what is possible. Don't worry about what's probable or what you think you deserve. Don't even consider what is most reasonable. From this moment, I'd like to welcome you to *dream*. What is your greatest next step? What would ideal health look like? What would emotional freedom feel like? If there were no limits or expectations, who would you be? In what ways would you be different? Is there anything (or everything) you could improve or take to another level of excellence?

Prepare for the End

Once you realize the power you have to change and sense the sprouting wings of the desire to rise above, something new will show up: fear, resistance, or perhaps other distressing emotions. Some changes will evoke a feeling so intense that it will be like the fear of death itself. This is something that I'll explore in more detail later on in this book, but for now, let's be clear: if you're reading this, then you're ready to take another step. The more powerful the step, the more honest and profound, then the more likely you are to meet the "terror" of true change.

When change is real, significant, and lasting, it will feel like the end of the world. That's because it *is!* It's the end of you as you understand yourself today. It may be hard to imagine, but when you look at it from this perspective, fear and resistance are good things. They are normal and indicate positive changes. So when you encounter these, pay attention and keep going.

If your experiences are always easy, then you're probably not moving beyond old patterns and limiting beliefs. Sometimes change hurts, and it's supposed to. This doesn't mean you should look for misery or try to inflict discomfort on yourself. More often than not, if you aren't happy with the present situation, it will require a period of discomfort—unknowing, anxiety, or impatience, for instance—before you see the light and feel the differences.

Many self-help authors, popular psychologists, and physicians agree that happiness is possible and doing what you love is a part of healing. This is true. However, the part that few people want you to know is that even doing what you love or finding inner peace can make you *uncomfortable* in the process.

If you feel challenged by the ideas and choices that follow, *good!* Take a deep breath, and remember that it may be the end of the world as you know it, but that's the point. Forge new paths, within and without; move beyond where you are; and welcome every possibility available to you.

> *"Live as if you were to die tomorrow. Learn as if you were to live forever."*
>
> — MAHATMA GANDHI

⊚ ⊚ ◉ ⊚ ⊚

CHAPTER THREE

Original Source: Where It All Started

"I ask you to look both ways. For the road to a knowledge of the stars leads through the atom; and important knowledge of the atom has been reached through the stars."

— SIR ARTHUR STANLEY EDDINGTON

Beyond the Stars

When did you last go out into the night to gaze at the stars? When did you last take the time, perhaps lying on an old blanket, supported by the nurturing earth, to do nothing but look into the darkness—your eyes straining to see further into the inky black ocean of sky? Nowhere else to be, you breathe easily and softly as the wind gently washes over your face. What did you observe? Where did that journey take you?

Like many children, I used to love to go outside at night and lie under the stars. As kids, some of us were fortunate enough to be able to have that adventure on a regular basis, and others remember those moments only as rare gems found on the occasional night walk to a park or during a weekend camping trip. But the experience is unforgettable.

If I close my eyes, I can still see the jeweled darkness, patterns and stories scattered across the heavens. I've often wondered who else was looking with me. How many generations before me had also admired this vast display? Did Jesus Christ walk beneath the same night sky? Did Buddha or Mohammed? What about Alexander the Great, Queen Elizabeth, Anne Frank, Lao-tzu, or Steve Biko? Did Galileo help find these stars?

Were the pyramids and the Great Wall of China built beneath this same moon? Was there a young Aboriginal man somewhere deep in the wild country of Australia sleeping alone beneath this same night sky on his first walkabout, his journey into manhood? Did he wait for that moon to chase away his fears, or did he savor the darkness as the stars surfaced by the millions? How many stories, births, and deaths took place beneath this majestic array of lights? And there I was, wondering . . . one more story, one more set of eyes. Beneath the mystery, I was one more soul pondering what lay beyond.

No matter how far I looked or how hard I thought about it, time and space raced on. *What was beyond the stars? There had to have been a starting point, and what was before that?* The soaring awareness was endless, and soon my mind would rest. Below the eternal sky, my thoughts would grow silent and my heart would open, like the most precious night-blooming flower. Only during those very rarest moments, something would shift, and effortlessly, I'd feel an opening within.

It's hard to put that experience into words, but if you've felt it (and most of us have at one point or another), then you understand. I glimpsed the solitary nature of my life's path and the fragility of my existence. I knew that no matter what my life would show, in time it would pass and be forgotten. All my suffering and all my triumphs would eventually vanish into the vastness of time. I am a mere blink in the life of a star.

In the same moment, however, there was a deep, deep peace and a profound sense of connection. No matter how insignificant I might feel as an individual, I am forever a part of something extraordinary. I share the same air, water, and sky as the highest and lowest of humanity. My breath is distantly intermingled with the exhalation of the jungles and great rain forests. My bones and blood are infused with the same carbon and chemicals found in all the plants, stones, and animals of the earth. Somehow, beneath the night sky, I knew that everything was and is connected. I could feel the love that all things emerged from and knew that we are all ultimately united. Oneness was the feeling. Oneness was the thought.

Those precious moments shaped me in subtle yet profound ways. The ability to step back and breathe in the grand design of life has always helped me weather the storms and seasons of change. I'm reminded not to take things too seriously, to practice humility and the art of letting go. It's a lifelong process, but the perspective assists my growth immeasurably.

In the Beginning

Where do we find the beginning of your life or any life? Birth? Conception? Adulthood? Your job? Place? History? Ancestry? The Garden of Eden? Protoplasm? The big bang?

It really doesn't matter what we believe about the origins of life because there's a single fact that unites us: it is a mystery. The fact that we're here at all is a total, mind-boggling mystery. No matter how far back you can imagine, the arrow of time continues infinitely. Before everything that exists today, there was a *Something* that no one really understands. Many people call it God or Spirit. Theologians and religious leaders fumble with metaphors and poetry to convey the extraordinary enigma that is God, the Creator of all things. This great mystery we come from is also called Emptiness, Energy, or Consciousness. There are literally thousands of religious, scientific, and cultural terms for the Source and Force of all that is, and each is just as limited as the next.

The world of science is no further ahead than the world of spirituality in explaining it all. Not only are we still hypothesizing whether the big bang theory adds up, but we don't really understand what exactly preceded that precious moment and where it all came from. The human mind can't fully grasp the notion of eternity or infinity. Something without end or beginning cannot be thought of at all. At best, the source of all life—the source of you—is glimpsed through feelings and fleeting experiences.

If you haven't thought much about the vastness of life, you can still experience it. Take the time to go out at night and look at the stars. Find a safe place where you can see them clearly—try your backyard, a park, a large unlit parking lot, or a weekend camping trip. Guess how many stars you see and how far into the distance they go. Then remember one thing: no matter how far you imagine, space goes even farther. No matter how long you think they've been in existence, they've been there long, long before. The stars will wake you up to a glimpse of eternity, and *that* is where we come from. It's a miracle.

The mysterious potential that turned itself into everything is the Source and Force behind all, and it's still at work. That energy, power, and potential never went away. It's here right now . . . in this book, in the ground beneath you, and in the air you're breathing. It is in *you*. You can never escape it—you're embraced by the miracle. Any way you look at it, you are a miracle, too.

Something Extraordinary

More than a million choices have led you to this moment, and more than a million choices of more than a million other people have set the stage, context, and circumstances of your life. Beyond that, there are more than a million other factors on Earth that have allowed you and every other human being in your lineage to survive—from the trees' constant production of oxygen to the plants and animals that have sustained you. Sunlight, water, and the endless turning seasons; flashing eyes, bones, and blood; dreams, despairs, and delights; you are a dancing particle of light in an infinite symphony of energy.

What does all of this mean? It means that you're a part of something much greater. No matter what you're experiencing right now, one thing is absolutely certain: you are an essential thread in the extraordinary fabric of life. You are not alone, and you're certainly not the first to face the decisions and situations that are before you. You're an expression of the mystery that life has emerged from; your life is a dance between your individuality *and* your connection.

You are unique among billions of humans, yet you share this world in a more intimate way than you can imagine. The power to create life, diversity, and the interconnection of all things lives within you. Love and connection is your essence and will always return you to that power and potential. Another word for the "felt experience" of love and connection is *Oneness*. That is the nature of our Original Source. It may sound complicated, but it's an important starting point. The sooner you understand Oneness, the sooner you'll be free from stress and can begin healing.

Oneness

"Eventually, you will come to understand that love heals everything, and love is all there is."

— GARY ZUKAV

Oneness is more than a concept; it's an experience and a way of living. If you can grasp this idea, the rest of your journey will be easier for you than it will be for others who have not. Oneness is what you understood when you were born. It's not a belief—rather, it's a way of being.

I remember when my wife carried our son, Narayan, inside her. His changes were hers, hers were his. When he was born, although physically separate, mother and son were still as one being. Their sleep and wake cycles were connected; their moods and awareness of each other always interplaying.

Shortly after Narayan was born, we asked our doctor whether it was dangerous for him to sleep in bed with us until he was a bit older. Would we roll over onto him and hurt him? The doctor laughed at the question, and so did our midwife and others we knew. Why? The answer was always the same: "Keep him next to you and don't worry—no sober mother would roll onto her newborn. They are so connected, so alert to each other's movements and emotions, that a dangerous collision is almost impossible." It certainly proved to be true.

Love and connection—Oneness—was how it all began for each of us. But the idea and practice of it was eventually taught out of us by our families, schools, society, and experiences. (We'll get to that fun transition in a chapter to come.)

Oneness is also one of the most shared concepts across the world's religious traditions. Written teachings about it have shown up throughout history. In every culture throughout time, there have been saints, mystics, sages, shamans, and prophets who have come to a common conclusion: all things in this world are deeply interconnected and, ultimately, are only diverse expressions of the one original Source Energy. This was the essential experience and conviction of most religious leaders. They called the Oneness of life different things, such as God, Allah, Hashem, The Great Mystery, and so on; but the idea is universal. Oneness means that we're each united with all of life.

From the classics texts of Aldous Huxley, Joseph Campbell, and Evelyn Underhill to the modern scholarship of Wayne Teasdale, Huston Smith, Andrew Harvey, and Deepak Chopra, the research and conclusion remains the same: the experience of Oneness transcends culture, class, and training. Anyone can directly feel and know the interconnection of life so deeply that it becomes a way of being.

This concept isn't just a spiritual or religious idea, however. It's now a clear scientific principle. Einstein devoted the last years of his life to attempting to prove the unified field theory, a belief that all of life and matter are united by an underlying energy or consciousness. The great quantum physicists David Bohm, Niels Bohr, Sir Arthur Stanley Eddington, Max Planck, and many others were convinced that at the very deepest (smallest) level of all things was an energy, universal in form and without end. Deep within each cell, molecule, atom, and nucleus—deep in the heart of matter—breathes an energy so subtle and yet so essential it could be called *spirit.*

The natural and earth scientists, such as environmentalists, biologists, meteorologists, and ecologists, are also convinced of this Oneness. There is too much evidence that the pollution in one part of the world impacts the climate, air, and water in another. The chemicals that the smallest animals eat from our waste and farming practices travel up the food chain until large doses of those chemicals appear in our daily diet. Changes in the habitat or population of any one creature send a ripple effect throughout the world. Oneness is the law of nature: what we do to others, we do to ourselves.

It's a big idea to grasp at first, but imagine it like this: think of the Force that preceded all of life as being like an ocean. At times, of course, the ocean freezes under certain conditions and forms ice. The ice is unlike the ocean—it floats upon it and doesn't even look like it. But eventually, the conditions change, and the ice melts back into the sea. Was it ever really different? Separate? Where did the ice go? Was the ocean "in" the ice? Or was it always one thing in many forms? Isn't your life similar?

This is how both mystics and quantum physicists think of life. You are like a beautiful iceberg floating on the ocean. You think you're separate from your origin, but you are one and the same. Even in your separateness, you place your attention on that which is above the water, never really taking stock of the incredible magnitude of your power, presence, and connection to all that surrounds you. For a while, you have form, and in time, you will not.

If you truly understood this, you wouldn't need to be told to be kind, nor would you need to be reminded to recycle, to forgive others, or to respect yourself. You would feel the hurt of those you harm. You'd be willing to go the extra mile to create understanding and shared prosperity. You'd know that everyone is related through this Oneness. We really are one family, one body, one mind. You wouldn't worry about who wins—you'd be sure that no one loses. You'd love others as yourself; you'd see the spark of something sacred in all things; and you'd know that every experience is a lesson, a chance to grow toward understanding the supremacy of Oneness.

From Cosmos to Conception

For many people, the contemplation of the vastness of the universe and our origin is just too much to start with. It sounds too philosophical. "How can I relate to planets and comets?" some might ask. "How am I like a flower or a dolphin or a mountain? It sounds too metaphysical!" or "How is this about *my* life?"

It is okay to return to this chapter and the idea and experience of Oneness later. The simple message is that your origin is extraordinary and so are you—you will always be much more than what you do, have, or think.

Take a moment to consider your birth. At one point, "you" were nothing more than a speck, an imperceptible speck that was really more energy than matter. You were smaller than the head of a pin—just a cluster of cells. From that hint of material, an entire human life unfolded. Now here you are walking, talking, driving, e-mailing, drinking coffee, and wondering about your life. You've come a long way.

Know that you are incredible, complex, and totally amazing. When you were a baby, people marveled at everything you did. Your smile, your wave, your first step, your first word—it was all so wonderful. Everything you did was precious. But once you did something a hundred times, then it wasn't so interesting, and everyone stopped seeing the miracle. Don't forget, though—it is *still* miraculous. The fact that you woke up today is amazing. The fact that you can read and understand language and ideas and recognize the opportunity to change is amazing. Gratitude and wonder are two of the most empowering and healing perspectives. These characteristics will change your life.

The ability to step back and put your life in perspective is a vital trait among those who escape Inspiration Deficit Disorder. Embracing mystery, humility, appreciation, and a sense of curiosity are hallmarks of resilient and happy people. Explore these four qualities and you will have already started to eliminate any inspiration deficits in your life. On the other hand, when you resist these qualities, you will eventually fall out of balance.

> *"Life is not a problem to be solved,*
> *but a mystery to be lived."*

— attributed to THOMAS MERTON

◉◉◉◉◉

CHAPTER FOUR

Your Essential Self: Understanding Your Vitality and Purpose

"We are the hero of our own story."

— MARY MCCARTHY

Born to Shine

As long as I live, I will never forget the moment my son was born. My wife, Monica, and I chose to have a home birth supported by midwives and nurses so that we could welcome our child in our own loving, familiar space. More significantly, it was my honor to be my wife's primary doula (birth coach) and support. We almost never lost physical contact once the contractions began in our living room that afternoon. Then later that night, in the loving energy and setting of our bedroom, my wife courageously and gracefully delivered our baby boy into the world. It was mind-blowing, terrifying, amazing, awesome, beautiful, and astonishing. It was the most magnificent experience of my life.

Just moments later—not even a minute after Narayan came into the world—he was in our arms. Lying on Monica's chest with my hand on his tiny back, he turned his head toward me as if he recognized my voice and opened his eyes for the first time. I can't know what it was that he intended or understood in that moment, but I do know what I felt. It was bigger than words can express, a love and connection so overwhelming and pure that it defies all speech, science, and religion. Nothing existed but that moment, and in that moment lived all moments.

The story of Narayan's birth spread quickly to our immediate families in New Mexico and Canada, and then on to our extended families in South Dakota, Africa, New Zealand, and beyond. The focus of the great news was a photo. It seemed that from the very first day he had begun to smile, but on the morning of Narayan's fourth day, his smile was clear and so obvious it was unmistakable. His expression was so content, so joyful, that we knew it was more than "gas" or an accident. Even though many people have said that babies don't smile until they're older, Narayan kept on smiling, and we captured it in a picture for all the world to see. The response was amazing.

People circulated the photo via e-mail, and many displayed it in their offices or put it on their cell phones. Even my friend and colleague Dr. Christiane Northrup began showing people the image in some of her presentations! One friend told me that whenever she felt sad or stressed-out, she'd just look at Narayan's smiling face and her mood would improve. Individuals I'd never met were actually using the photo to motivate themselves and feel uplifted.

Why all this fuss about a picture? And what does all this have to do with *you?*

The photo revealed two simple things: First, that a person's personality (such as Narayan's, which is still sunny and full of smiles) is clear from the very beginning. Second, it showed that the natural essence a person is born with is so pure, so beautiful, and so true that when we simply witness that essence of another, it connects us more deeply to ourselves, as well as to something greater. Some call it God, and others refer to it as the mystery of life. Most of us can agree to call it our Original Source. When we touch that pure source, all of our everyday troubles melt away. We are healed by authenticity—what is real and genuine—and that's why the photo of a smiling four-day-old baby could inspire and heal so many. The beauty of your essence never changes. Those who live and express their essence are beautiful, no matter what they look like.

You Came with Instructions

It's hard to imagine, but if you have any recollection of being a young child or if you've raised a child, you know that we all come into this world with everything we need to be happy and free. No one has to teach children how to play or be curious or full of energy. They show up like that. The essence of self is in place from day one and contains all the energy, wisdom, talent, and drive a person needs to live fully and well. Much the same can be said of caring for animals and plants. The challenge in raising children lies not in what you give them, but in being careful about what you take away.

People use a range of terms when talking about the Essential Self, including *essence, true self, soul,* and *authentic self.* I often interchange them for variety, and also because not everyone will connect with the same term equally. Regardless of how we name it, when I discuss this idea of original self (Essential Self) with groups, people always respond quickly with examples. Their understanding is intuitive and immediate. During a recent workshop I led, I asked the group, "Do any of you remember what you used to love to do as a child, and has it remained a passion to this day?" Most people could think of something they loved to do when they were young, such as paint, ride horses, play basketball, knit, look for stones in nature, write, and so on. I try to emphasize that those natural tendencies are examples of their Essential Self. When people talk about these essential elements, they light up with the joy of the memory and energy of enthusiasm. If we can spend more time doing the things we love, we can find our way back to the center of self again.

In that same workshop, a man and a woman in the audience raised their hands to speak. The gentleman offered, "As long as I can remember, I've loved to build things. Even as a toddler, my parents said that I'd sit with building blocks for hours. Then it was LEGO bricks, and as I got older, I'd use whatever I could get my hands on." I asked him if he'd considered some kind of hobby that would involve building—perhaps carpentry or design. He laughed, saying, "I'm an architect, and I own an international construction company. We specialize in unique and innovative designs. I swear I got some of my best ideas from when I was a kid."

Then the woman who had raised her hand spoke, saying, "I've always loved dancing. As soon as I could walk, they say I tried to dance! I took whatever lessons my parents could afford and practiced any type of dance moves I saw on TV. When I was in college, I ended up studying business and eventually became an office manager. My parents were so happy! They didn't want me to be a starving artist. But you know what?" She paused and looked around the room with conviction before continuing. "I *hated* it. I couldn't stand being a manager, and I quit after five awful, draining years. Before I did, though, I took night classes to become a dance instructor. It was a lot of work, but once I left my day job, I went right back to dancing and haven't stopped since. It's been ten years, and I've loved every minute of it— even the challenges and financial debt, which I'm now finally coming out of. It's been hard . . . but amazing. Before this change, life was *just* hard."

I love these stories, and most of us probably know people like this as well. We know that when someone follows his or her passion, joy and resilience follows. Not all of us can make a career out of what inspires us, but we can all build an inspired life from the foundations of our talents, interests, gifts, and sense of purpose. Some of us inspire and feed our Essential Self through hobbies, some through community roles, and others through volunteering or spiritual practice. There are so many ways to invigorate that core self we were born as. If we pay attention to what we like to do on our favorite and most meaningful vacations and what "just being ourselves" looks like, we'll begin to notice themes from our childhood and ideas for the future.

I've met many successful businessmen who in their last attempt to find health and meaning felt forced to admit that they had given up everything they loved to do because it didn't make sense or money. Interestingly, several such men who have approached me with their stories were once surfers. Imagine a man whose greatest delight is spending hours in the sun and water, playing, exploring, laughing, and living in the moment. Then imagine the same man wearing a suit and tie, and spending nearly every hour of every day inside a building. Imagine what it would feel like to completely give up your surfboard for a life of planning, controlling, and trying to make something happen. How could that not feel like a deep and painful betrayal of the Essential Self? Rather than admitting the betrayal, most simply buried themselves deeper in work.

The Soul's Code

More than vocation and recreation, the soul provides a code that is also essential to your health. Everything from the music that soothes you to the type of ice cream you like and the spiritual practices that work for you is imprinted in your essence. Don't be fooled by family or community. More often than not, when you feel like you don't fit in, the answer isn't to try harder, but to find your own way with balance and respect for the people, places, and things you love.

When you express your truth through your choices, health and happiness will follow. Quite literally, a life disconnected from the Essential Self is one doomed to stress, unhappiness, and poor health. The *energy* of the self is a very real life force that infuses the entire human system, uniting body, mind, and emotion. *When the essence of self is not honored, the energy for living is diminished.* This is when the roots of Inspiration Deficit Disorder begin to take hold. The lesson of the child and the Essential Self is that your greatest joy and vitality lie in honoring what makes you unique. Your tendencies, preferences, and passions are your links to your best experience of life. They are your way back to Original Source.

Honoring Your Self

My mother created an interesting family tradition around our birthdays. Looking back, it may seem a bit indulgent and silly when carried far into adulthood, but on second thought, it's a simple yet profound example of honoring the soul and affirming the Essential Self.

Every year, for as long as my siblings and I can remember, my mom would ask the birthday boy or girl to choose the meal for the evening (sometimes the whole day, too). We could pick anything she could make, and everyone else would enjoy the meal with us. We also got to decide on the activities for the day—whatever we loved to do. To top it off, there was a surprise theme.

When the table was set, the guest of honor had to be off somewhere else playing until everything was ready. The themes varied, but the one thing they had in common was that they always affirmed one of our passions, talents, or interests. So it could be as simple as an animal theme for me, hockey for my brother, or waterskiing for my sister, for example. Less often it was something featuring musicians from a favorite band or the characters from a TV show or movie; if it spoke to *who* we were as individuals, then it would be included.

What is significant is that these "theme parties" didn't end when we became teenagers, or even adults. I understand now that this idea wasn't just about making the room cheery and fun; all of my mom's efforts were to affirm that our family knew and honored every member. It was an "essence day" celebration more than anything else. As an adult, I've had themes such as "writing/being an author," "Africa," and even "dreamwork"—all things that are an important part of my life today.

Essence Day

In many ways, this practice of honoring the essence of a person during a birthday is really a return of an ancient rite of passage. It is ceremonial and mythic, and it supports self-love and self-esteem. The majority of people save the more meaning-based celebrations for "special" birthdays, graduations, or monumental anniversaries. But what would happen if we honored each other in that way every year? If instead of focusing on the drinks or the cake or the popularity contest, what if we focused on the spirit of that person and all that makes him or her unique? In a way, we'd move from *birthday* to *essence day*.

This might be a challenge for Hallmark, but it could be easy for *you* to embrace. The shift moves from focusing on what you can buy for someone to what you can't buy: creativity, individuality, or eccentricity. Typically, my mother's themes involved the skill and support of the rest of the family to help make decorations. From time to time, we might have used some prefab party dinnerware (the likes of which were designed by Disney or Warner Bros.), but for the most part, everything was homemade.

In contrast, a typical birthday party might be centered on Harry Potter or *Golf Digest* and the use of certain colors—not on the essence of the individual being celebrated. What is important to remember is that the theme should be defined by the guest of honor, not by a TV character or film star. That's not a theme— that's a commercial. When you celebrate Essence Day, your focus is on all the things that make the person unique. The way it looks and how well you've pulled it all together is really a secondary matter.

An Old Tradition

In many Indigenous cultures throughout the world— which includes my friends and extended family in the Lakota Sioux community—there is a long-standing practice of honoring people. More than awards or prizes, there is a tradition of holding ceremonies to celebrate and recognize the character and accomplishments of individuals. Stories are told, songs are sung, and an affirmation of the essence of who they are is expressed.

My mentor Wanagi Wachi once said to me, "Sometimes I think your culture has it backward. For you, funerals are the time and place where people say the most wonderful things about their family and friends. It's the time when people really try to show how much that person who passed meant to them. But at that point, they're really just saying it for themselves or for the community to hear. We believe that the individual should be honored while they are alive."

How Do You Honor Your Essence?

Even more important than other people honoring your essence is for you to honor yourself. Look at your bedroom, bathroom, car, or office. Is it filled with things that tell the story of who you are? Does it remind you of your essence even on days when you don't feel it?

Perhaps it's someone else's idea of beautiful, clean, or ideal. Be sure to fill your life with touchstones, reminders of your Authentic Self. You don't have to act childish or overindulgent, but you can be childlike and purposeful. Where there is meaning and healthy affirmation, there is joy and vitality.

The Soul of Health—the Health of the Soul

"When you move toward that which is most fulfilling and life-enhancing—with joy and pleasure—healing follows."

— CHRISTIANE NORTHRUP, M.D.

The amazing thing about the Essential Self is that it not only knows what makes us happy, but it's also what makes us healthy. A number of important research studies and books have been written on this subject. Popular medical doctors such as Bernie Siegel, Christiane Northrup, Mehmet Oz, and Mimi Guarneri often refer to a great deal of cutting-edge research that shows that being happy is a precursor to being healthy. The very state of being content releases vital chemicals into the body while triggering a number of physiological reactions that actually promote well-being. You can find more evidence and research in the works of microbiologist Dr. Bruce Lipton; immunologist Dr. Candace Pert; psychologist Dr. Dan Baker; and physicians Dean Ornish, Andrew Weil, Harold Koenig, and Larry Dossey.

What all of the aforementioned experts and thousands of others have finally begun to embrace in Western medicine is a principle common to the world's ancient spiritual traditions: *the Essential Self must be honored and fed throughout life.* Otherwise, stress, despair, and illness will follow. Heal the soul and you'll have the greatest capacity to heal the whole. Address only the physical and you'll always struggle to find the most potent missing factor in wellness.

Whatever situation you may find yourself in, seek the most authentic response. This means that you honor your basic nature, which includes your essential gifts, talents, preferences, and passions. Seek the highest good, and be true to yourself.

My favorite popular example of the medicine of the soul is found in the work of Bernie Siegel, who was the assistant clinical professor of surgery at Yale. An accomplished surgeon and physician educator, Siegel's outlook changed dramatically in the 1970s when he observed that the number one predictor of successful recovery from cancer (as well as other conditions he treated) wasn't typical medical procedures or pharmaceuticals, but deep self-love and positive lifestyle changes that emphasized the unique essence of patients.

In 1978, Dr. Siegel started Exceptional Cancer Patients, which explored art, emotions, dreams, and community to help people engage the healing power of their natural essence. His books—such as *Love, Medicine & Miracles*—have changed the lives of thousands. What he has learned in the operating rooms and clinical settings of some of the nation's most prestigious hospitals and universities is that healing is ultimately a mysterious endeavor rooted more in the unexplainable essence of each person than many of us will ever realize or admit.

Stories of Transformation

My understanding of the healing power of authenticity has come through my own life and in my work with people facing and seeking change. To see the price that individuals pay for living with a lack of inspiration and integrity has been astonishing. And to witness the positive transformative power that emerges when these same individuals simply learn to honor and love themselves has been humbling and uplifting.

Tim

For example, I remember Tim, the CEO of a Fortune 500 company, who was very successful but very unsatisfied. He possessed money and power, and had a wonderful family—everything you could imagine. But he treated the people around him poorly and spent all of his time focused on achieving further financial success. He ended up with a heart condition, a failing marriage, and difficulty facing the substantial guilt and regret that had grown within him. He was estranged from his parents and siblings, always too busy to connect.

Eventually, Tim sold his company, started therapy, and took a year off to travel with his wife and children. When he returned, he became a satisfied *and* successful president of a nonprofit business aimed at cleaning up much of the waste that his old company and others like it had generated over the years.

Sarah

Sarah found herself turning 45, working obsessively at a job she felt controlled and overwhelmed by. She was in a terrible trap, as she had little time for herself or a social life. When she took time off—only because she was sick—she felt painfully sad and lonely, which drove her to spend even more hours at the office. Her work wasn't fulfilling, but her home life was even worse.

She couldn't remember when, but at some point, the only thing that her home and work life had in common was that she got drunk every chance she could. Business dinners and lunches were natural excuses, and winding down at the end of a long day was another good reason to have a few drinks. Her health was failing even though she seemed "together" to those around her. Inside, however, she was slowly dying as she unsuccessfully battled what had become a fierce addiction.

We had an honest conversation, which quickly revealed the pain of her childhood with an alcoholic mother and a cruel, critical father whom she always tried to please and appease. Her current situation was just a replay of all the old hurts and lessons from the past. What she wanted, she confessed to me, was to be a writer, move away from the city, and live a simple life—maybe even learn how to grow fruits and vegetables.

Sarah's miracle was that once she left her job, sold her house, and moved to the coast of South Carolina as she'd always imagined, her plan to get help with her addiction was no longer necessary. Her plan "fell apart" because the urge to escape her life ended when she began to both love herself and honor the things she truly enjoyed. Her drinking problem simply ceased to exist. She still e-mails me from time to time with updates about her garden.

Greg

Then there was Greg, who denied his homosexuality all his life. Ashamed as a result of his parents' values and views, he was convinced that being gay was a choice—that is, something he could control and change. After building a life complete with a loving wife, children, and a wildly successful business, he became very ill. Greg was diagnosed with depression and cancer. He told me that it felt like his lie was eating him alive.

In time, he recognized that he couldn't change who he was born to be and finally confessed the truth to his wife. He began to work hard to transform his life, bestowing honesty and respect upon everyone he loved. Not all, but nearly everyone he knew decided to support him. Soon, he and his wife even became the best of friends. Strangely, his cancer vanished along with his depression after only the first stage of his treatment.

"The art of healing comes from nature, not from the physician. Therefore the physician must start from nature, with an open mind."

— PARACELSUS

Finding the Cure

These are just a few examples of Inspiration Deficit Disorder and the physical *and* emotional transformations that are possible (you'll read about more in later chapters). For many people, the stakes aren't so high. Some stories of change are much simpler and less complicated: a return to school, new friends, the beginning of a spiritual practice, or the end of an old habit, for instance. Sometimes healing occurs from changes within a job or relationship, or perhaps it's moving to a new place or redecorating an old one.

Interestingly enough, it's often not what we must *stop* doing so much as what we must *start* doing. It may begin with setting firm limits about how we spend our time with friends, family, or work. It always means that we pay attention to our energy, assessing how we use it and restore it.

What all of the individuals in the previous examples have in common is that they suffered from Inspiration Deficit Disorder. Clearly, the symptoms can vary depending on the person and situation, but the root is consistently a disconnection from the Essential Self. What unites all these stories of resilience and extraordinary change is the honoring of the heart by embracing truth and authenticity. The cure for Inspiration Deficit Disorder is always the same in principle, although it may look different for each person.

Essential Energy

"The important thing in science is not so much to obtain new facts as to discover new ways of thinking about them."

— SIR WILLIAM LAWRENCE BRAGG

This essence, or soul, is more than just your personality, sense of purpose, and talents—it's your connection to your inner power. Much of the modern research into the essence of self suggests an extraordinary mind-body connection. Researchers have been forced to speculate that the human self and mind is actually made up of energy, a subtle but real vital force that holds all this information about who you're meant to be.

Gary Schwartz discusses the laboratory-based evidence for a measurable "energy body" in his books *The Energy Healing Experiments* and *The Living Energy Universe*. Deepak Chopra also draws much attention to this research, as does Larry Dossey, particularly in a great work of his called *Recovering the Soul: A Scientific and Spiritual Search*. For larger overviews about the modern scientific case for the energy of the self, see *Vibrational Medicine* by Richard Gerber, M.D.; the anthology *Measuring the Immeasurable;* and the incredible annotated bibliographies of energy-based healing approaches by Dr. Daniel Benor.

These scientifically based reviews highlight hundreds of studies that strongly support the assertion that each human being possesses a life force that runs throughout the body, much the way a computer is animated by electricity that courses through every function and facet. This is a fact of life that most modern quantum physicists would accept. Physics has long held the notion that all things are reducible, on some level, to nothing but energy. Energy is all that is.

> *"Individuality is only possible if it unfolds from wholeness."*
>
> — DAVID BOHM

Something We Always Knew: Watch Your Language!

Although new to most people in the modern world, many cultures have never lost the belief in a human vital force. Ancient civilizations had words to describe this sacred self and the energy that it was composed of. Indigenous and Eastern traditions have also maintained the belief in a vital force, referring to it as *chi, ki, qi,* and *prana* (think "tai chi"). Unfortunately, in the West, we have long forgotten the complexity of the soul and the natural vital force that is our essence. Yet this fact of life is so pronounced, so strong and real, that we all know what this energy feels like. We are "energy beings," and we interact with the world as such.

For example, all of us have walked into a room at one time or another and immediately "sensed" an energy we liked or disliked. We hear things like, "Oh, I love the *energy* in here," or "I'm not sure who was here before us, but it doesn't *feel* good." We talk about individuals who drain us, and others who inspire and energize us. We exclaim that we're *jazzed, amped, revved up,* or that we've received a *boost.* We comment that someone has *good vibes* or that we don't like a person's *vibe.* We even say things such as, "I'll *send* love," "Send me good energy," "That night was electric," or "I felt the energy of the crowd." We use these specific words and phrases because we were born with an energy dimension to our body and soul, and it stays with us until our last breath.

Understanding the energy of the self is important as you move forward into understanding how you got to where you are today. Much of it has to do with how you've responded to and managed the energy in your life. Your current health and the degree to which you're content and feel vital all have to do with this aspect, as you'll soon see. Inside you is a force untouched by the events and dramas of life. You may be confused in thought or hurt by your emotional experiences, but your essence remains pure, and your inner power lies waiting to be tapped.

As I've mentioned, my mentor Wanagi Wachi was a healer and spiritual teacher. When he offered his counsel to individuals seeking healing, he would always remind them:

> *"There is something within you that is greater than anything that was ever said or done to you. As soon as you remember that, then you are not the hurt, stress, chaos, or confusion of your life—these are only feelings and passing experiences. They are not you. When you know that, there's hope. Knowing you are a spirit [energy and essence] is enough to give you the space you need to examine your life and seek a deeper experience."*

Take a look at the following figure, which will help you visualize the first two aspects of self. Use it to begin to map your own inner landscape. As you progress, the figure will grow and change, and so will your understanding of your own essence.

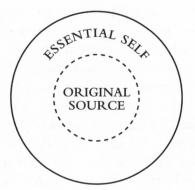

Now that you've been told that you already know everything you need in order to find peace, power, and purpose, it leads to new questions: If we are in fact beings of energy; potential; and natural, self-healing wisdom—what happened? How did we get from love and connection to fear and reaction? How does that great vigor and wisdom become so wildly out of view, so painfully out of reach?

We'll examine the answers in the next chapter and come to understand what the Wall of Wounding is and the role it plays in our lives.

◎◎◉◎◎

CHAPTER FIVE

The Wall of Wounding: How Life Shapes Us

"I wonder if any of them can tell from just looking at me that all I am is the sum total of my pain, a raw woundedness so extreme that it might be terminal. It might be terminal velocity, the speed of the sound of a girl falling down to a place from where she can't be retrieved. What if I am stuck down here for good?"

— ELIZABETH WURTZEL

What Happened?

The extraordinary power and wisdom of your essence is beyond description. Its beauty, potential, and resilience are unimaginable. When you become aware of these truths, new questions begin to emerge. "If *everyone* is so wonderful, connected, and miraculous, how did *I* end up like this? And why is the world such a mess?"

It's a basic, unavoidable fact: if you were born and raised on planet Earth, then you've got some personal history to deal with. Some people call it skeletons in the closet, and psychologists refer to it as the result of your "formative years" or "family-of-origin issues." Twelve steppers talk about defects of character and moral inventories, and the famous psychologist Carl Jung spoke of the "shadow," but it all adds up to the same simple reality: *any experiences early in life that were felt to betray, threaten, or attack your Essential Self are wounding.* Because you come from Oneness (love and connection), anything that feels like disconnection or creates the opposite impulse (fear and disconnection) is painful. Such episodes can occur at any time but have the deepest impact when they take place early in life.

The trouble with these wounding experiences is that they create an emotional energy that becomes rooted in the body and a story or idea of how the world works that lives on in the mind. These two powerful things, the emotion and energy of wounding, must be faced, felt, and freed; or they will become *unknowingly* integrated into who you think you are and how you think your life "should" unfold.

I'd like to share a personal account that will give you an example of the ways in which someone's old beliefs or patterns can affect various aspects of life. My experience may not be something you can relate to, but it conveys many of the themes of Inspiration Deficit Disorder and how it can be resolved.

Mr. Good Hits the Wall

By the time I was in my 20s, I was already on my way to working as a healer and teacher. As I describe in my book *Return to The Sacred,* I had begun a deep search into the world of health, healing, and spirituality as a young teenager. By 21, I'd already researched and even trained in certain forms of alternative medicine and counseling.

I had taken introductory psychology classes while I was in college, studied intimately with a Native American healer, attended workshops on addiction counseling, explored shamanic approaches to healing, and tried every kind of modern and ancient healing model and practice that crossed my path. I was clear about my mission to help others and had always been known as a compassionate person, someone with good intentions and a good head on his shoulders. It was a way of life and a self-concept that worked for me. Then I fell in love.

I look back now with the deepest of respect for the woman who helped me totally unravel my life. We had a strong love connection, and a kind of tragic contract to bring each other to the edge of life as we knew it. There was a timing and circumstance that allowed me to learn a great deal about what I now call the Wall of Wounding.

Marina (not her real name) and I met at a New Year's Eve party. I was studying in Arizona, she in North Dakota. We happened to be at the same event in our common hometown of Winnipeg, Canada, while on vacation. It was a brief encounter, but sparks flew and we dove into an epic long-distance relationship. In many ways, our commitment to each other and the intensity of our relationship unfolded too quickly. We didn't really know each other very well when we promised to make it work against the odds.

After a year of a few passionate visits and endless phone calls, letters, and packages in the mail (this was before e-mail), we decided to move in together. This required us to find a city we could both agree to live in; and a university where both of us could still pursue our studies. It all felt very romantic at the time. We moved in together despite having never lived in the same place before; nor had we ever seen each other face stress, success, or family issues. All of our experiences of each other were clouded by the rosy hue that surrounds anything that is more fantasy than reality.

A Turn of Events

Only a few days into our new life—in our new apartment and new hometown—the phone rang and an old friend of mine called to congratulate me on the move and on the relationship. This friend also happened to be a former girlfriend. Now I know that new relationships can be offset or threatened by old ones, even when intellectually we know that the old one ended for a reason. What followed this call, however, was something far beyond what a little fear can explain. Marina quickly went into a downward spiral of jealousy, self-doubt, fear, withdrawal, and low energy. It was as if someone she loved had died—violently.

But love perseveres! I felt that I probably deserved some of the emotional attacks. I thought that perhaps I should have cut off all my ties to past girlfriends and that I wasn't being sensitive to Marina's feelings. I was afraid to lose her, worried I had failed her already. I wanted to believe this was a passing phase that had a lot to do with the stress of moving. A week or so later, we made up and felt more connected than ever. What a relief for both of us! The relationship went on, and we both survived. I knew then that being the good guy was all it took. Love would overcome—until the next episode, which followed shortly after.

I could fill the rest of this book with stories of the next *two years* of my life with Marina, including recollections of her deep waves of depression, the endless emotional attacks on me, the acts of self-harm, and the weeklong trip to the psychiatric hospital that followed a nervous breakdown in our living room. My efforts to soothe and help her were always short-lived. Accompanying her mood swings were constant fits of insecurity, jealousy, and doubt regarding my love and commitment. The more I tried, the more I questioned myself and felt like a failure.

I could also fill pages recounting my shock when I discovered that prior to our meeting, Marina had engaged in spells of drug abuse and a reckless lifestyle. I learned that her childhood was filled with severe abuse in many forms. I used to try to count the "good days" we had together, but to no avail. It was typically only a matter of two to three days before one cycle of emotion would end and another would begin.

Wasn't Love Enough?

I won't say that it was all a horror because in truth, we did love each other deeply and had many "highs" together. We also shared quite a bit in common. Marina was a talented, loving, intelligent, and beautiful woman; and there was something that made it nearly impossible for me to consider leaving her. And it wasn't just her threats of suicide.

Our crazy life remained largely a secret from all the distant family and friends who only got to see us during the holidays. I was becoming depleted and frustrated beyond belief, as if I were slowly dying from the inside out. It was strange and scary. I had always been a naturally happy and spiritually minded person until that time in my life. I'd never experienced such emptiness before and felt like I was being consumed by a horrible disease of the soul.

I look back and often laugh at my desire to drink myself to death—if only I actually drank! Being a "good guy," I had no major vices to numb the pain . . . although the thought of hiring a hit man as if I were on one of the mob shows on TV was looking more and more appealing. Finally, around the beginning of year two, it occurred to me that maybe my young, limited healing skills weren't enough to mend this woman's mind, nor was just being the good guy going to somehow transform the relationship. Was it possible that love *wasn't* enough? Maybe *I* needed help in order to help her.

Dr. Brown's Advice

Not long after my realization, I went to see a psychologist at my university's counseling center. Looking back, I was fortunate to have landed in the comfy office chair of one of the more experienced and respected therapists there. My first session was unforgettable. For the first time in more than a year, I had someone to confide in about the madness in my home life. At last I could tell someone about Marina and find out what I could do to help her.

After nearly a full hour explaining everything that had gone on and just how broken I thought Marina was, I asked—hoped—for something to help her. I also needed validation for myself and asked the doctor, "Is it just me, or is she a total mess?"

Dr. Brown had been listening intently and gave me a sympathetic smile. He took a deep breath and said a few simple things I'll never forget: "Well, she sounds like a very troubled young woman. There is no question that she needs professional help; and yes, it sounds complex and serious. It's not something you alone can fix as her partner." I sighed deeply with relief upon hearing this. I inwardly knew that the situation was too much to handle, and I could finally stop blaming myself for not being or doing enough.

Then Dr. Brown continued, saying, "What I'd like to know is what you're still doing in the relationship? Didn't it occur to you a year ago that you might want to get out? Or that it wasn't healthy? I can hear all that's 'wrong' with Marina, but I'd like to know more about what is going 'wrong' with *you*. What would keep you in a situation like that?"

For a moment, my world froze.

I had come face-to-face with my own Wall of Wounding. From a distance, my role seemed like a mystery. I thought, *Me, wounded? I was the healthy one! The good guy.* But then again, I knew that Dr. Brown was making a valid point. If I was so unhappy, why did I stay? If it wasn't a healthy situation, what was I doing fostering it?

Before I left his office that day, Dr. Brown gave me some homework. "Marina has kept you isolated and without support," he said. "The next time she says that you can't spend time with someone from school because she's afraid to be left alone—wondering if you're talking about her or perhaps scared that she might hurt herself—you need to go out anyway. She survives when you're at class or at the store. Why not just tell her you need to have a life? What do you think would happen?"

Then it hit me, and I mean like a truckload of bricks. If Marina said she needed my help and I said no, I was sure the world would explode, destroying everything and everyone in it. All of creation would come to a halt. The outcome of refusing her would be so horrific that I couldn't begin to face the fear, shame, guilt, powerlessness, and anxiety it would cause within me! I said all of this to Dr. Brown and then took a deep breath.

He looked at me for a moment and then simply asked, "Really? Do you *really* think the world will end if you do something good for yourself? I think we should find out." He glanced down at his watch and remarked that our time was up. "Come back next week and let me know." Then he joked lightly, "If the world explodes, I guess we won't need our next appointment."

I Give Myself Permission

It was a cold early spring day when I left Dr. Brown's office and began walking back to the apartment where Marina was waiting. I felt sick and confused, shaky with fear and anxiety. I knew I had to consider a new way of being. There was a guy in one of my classes I'd joked around with and often thought that if I were to have a friend from school that year, he might be one. Maybe I could ask him if he wanted to hang out, but the thought of *her* reaction made my stomach turn again.

As I approached our front door, my mouth went dry and a rush of self-talk ran through my mind: *Don't be cruel. What if you ruin her? How could you be such an asshole!* But I managed to push those thoughts aside and greet Marina. Then I explained that I had gone to see a counselor. At first she panicked, asking me why I'd want to talk about her with someone else, but I assured her that I was there to better myself—not to bad-mouth her. She relaxed and seemed generally supportive.

"He said," I stammered, "that it might help me to make a friend or two at school—guys, of course." I cringed as if waiting to be hit.

Marina paused. It was a long pause. "You know how I get when you talk about meeting new people," she said, as her voice grew panicky. I prepared to retreat, but then she continued. "Well, it's probably a good idea. Just give me a little warning. It *is* stupid that I can't let you have friends."

And that was it—I was free to try something new! A week later, I made plans to get a cup of tea with Jim, the guy from my class . . . but there was still another challenge to face.

The morning I was supposed to meet Jim, Marina freaked out and asked if I could postpone it. She wasn't ready, she explained, and said she might hurt herself if she thought I was talking about her or making plans to leave her. I realized that I was still stuck on her permission, hooked on her approval. However, I knew what was best for both of us, and as hard as it was, I went out anyway. Jim wasn't only a quick and natural companion, but he eventually became a lifelong ally and one of the best friends I've ever had.

The world did not explode that day.

Welcome to the Wall of Wounding

Behind any idea that's difficult to give up—whether it's embedded in a bad habit, old story, or reaction—are emotions and energies that keep you stuck. When you try to change, the unresolved issues show up and make you resort to old ways of thinking and behaving. It's important to realize that anything you want to modify or improve right now will involve dealing with and resolving these emotional energies in some way.

It doesn't matter how old the energy is or when it was first put into place. When that part of your Wall is triggered, it feels as real and powerful as the day it showed up. As you will see later on in this book, understanding this aspect is critical. When you begin to make major life changes, the energy of your Wall of Wounding will have to be assessed and addressed.

The Wall isn't typically felt until the patterns it has created are confronted or challenged. Then when you touch it, like a high-voltage electric fence, you remember what it's made of. The feelings will be intense.

As I continued to explore the poor decisions and cycles of codependency in my relationship with Marina, I realized that my present was being driven by my past. While parents are really *not always* the source of our greatest wounds (and are never to *blame* for our wounds), they almost always play an important or major role in how our Wall is formed. In my case, I discovered that I was replaying old emotions and stories from my home life. I had been blessed with a truly amazing family and a wonderful childhood that was dominated by happy memories, opportunities, and unconditional support. I had never before thought to look into the magic garden of my youth for poison apples . . . but there they were.

As I talked with Dr. Brown, I recounted many painful memories of arguments and interactions between my parents. I recalled a vivid time when I was about four years old. I heard my parents talking loudly in one room, not realizing it might be a brewing argument. I snuck into the kitchen to hide under the desk by the phone, hoping to surprise them. I used to love to jump out and surprise my unsuspecting family members—a game that lots of children play. That night, however, the game wasn't so fun.

Before I could push the chair out and yell "Surprise!" my mom and dad stormed into the room. It seemed that maybe my dad was following my mom, and their loud voices had escalated into a full-blown argument. Both were hollering at each other, and my dad, as he tended to, became the dominant, angry voice. I don't recall what he said or even what it was all about, but I distinctly remember his rage, his verbal attack, and my mother's helplessness. To me as a child, he seemed so cruel; she seemed so powerless; and I was confused, sad, fearful, and trapped. I was paralyzed by my emotions.

Later that night, after the war was over and I crawled out of my foxhole, I saw my mom crying in their bedroom. She assured me that everything was okay, but that "Dad was mean," and something about how she didn't deserve it. Mom went on about his cruelty. In retrospect, I can't imagine what she "should" have said to me, but that was the beginning of an emotional experience that *didn't* affirm my sense of love and connection. Rather, it fed my sense of fear and disconnection. It felt like neither of my parents were operating from their soul, and I certainly had to learn how to restore balance quickly. In the moment, all I knew was that I didn't want to have that awful feeling again.

Over time, a number of scenes at home affirmed the fear that somehow the world wasn't just, and that I needed to fix it. If I were the "good kid," if I put the women in my life first and my needs second—something my dad couldn't do—perhaps I could make things right. I also internalized the message that my mom needed unconditional support and my dad was the "bad guy." Clearly, in my young mind, his energy and actions needed to be overcome. The more I exposed and explored the roots of my emotions with Dr. Brown, the less power their energy had over me, and the freer I was to make new choices.

The most significant part of my story about my relationship with Marina occurred when I felt that the world would collapse around me if I dared to break the routine. The Wall of Wounding is the energy *and* emotion behind the old beliefs, patterns of behavior, and life scripts, as some people call them. The reaction I had as I faced my own Wall was physical, irrational, and emotional. The energy of my essence had been encased in a new energy—a shell I formed as a child.

Let's take a look at the diagram again. The next stage of development has been added, so it now looks like this:

Who Builds the Wall of Wounding?

If you return to the idea that everyone is born out of love and connection and arrives with a special essence, then the biggest threats are the things that don't feel like love and connection (whatever doesn't affirm your Essential Self). My previous example illustrates the power of old emotions that can resurface later in life and lead you to make poor choices. However, that experience barely touches the depth of pain, rejection, ridicule, and trauma that many people endure at a young age at the hands of their parents (or other family members), friends, teachers, or others.

Sexual, physical, or verbal abuse, as well as abandonment and addiction, for example, are much more common than most of us know or care to admit. Unfortunately, the odds are that we've experienced something like this firsthand or know someone who has.

As children, until we collide with a life experience that rejects our Essential Self, vitality and freedom flow easily into all areas of life. The tricky thing is that the Wall of Wounding is a natural response. It can be thought of as an unconscious way to protect the soul and remember what hurt so it can be avoided in the future. Starting at a young age, all experiences lead to either building our Walls or detracting from them. They are largely created by factors beyond our control.

Other Elements of the Wall

Some cultures I've experienced and studied, such as Hinduism, Buddhism, and certain Native American traditions, believe that we're born with "karmic" elements to our Wall. This means that in addition to showing up with our perfect Essential Self, we also carry unique fears and emotional energies that were either unresolved in past lives or inherited through the energetic memory of our ancestors. Therefore, a legacy of genocide, trauma, or violence may be unknowingly passed from one family member to another until it becomes conscious and intentionally healed.

The whole idea behind the pursuit of enlightenment in many traditions, Christianity included, is the absolute removal and purification of the Wall of Wounding. By doing so, our essence may be revealed and transcended in order to uncover the Original Source, or Pure Consciousness, that resides within us all. I truly believe there's something important to learn from these perspectives.

The modern therapeutic approach of "constellation therapy" also shares some powerful techniques and perspectives on healing the energy of imbalance that lives in families and communities. This "new" form of treatment draws on spiritual principles, modern psychology, and a range of innovative group exercises that address healing the Wall of Wounding in a way that acknowledges the impact of family of origin, as well as the energy and patterns of ancestors, rather than solely focusing on the individual's experiences. (You can learn more about this at **www.hellinger.com** [choose the English version of the site] and at the site of one of my colleagues: **www.johndore.com**.)

For some, these ideas may sound too metaphysical to be comfortable. You can work with the Inspiration Deficit Disorder model of growth whether or not you add the karmic and intergenerational element. The way you transform can be used and reused throughout your life. As a framework for thinking and awareness, the techniques in this book are flexible and can accommodate new learning or information and spiritual perspectives as you encounter them.

My ideas about the Wall of Wounding aren't entirely new. Much of this approach is just a simplified version of what most healers and therapists in the world would corroborate. Other elements I discuss, such as the focus on energy, are less commonly understood. What unites our understanding of the Wall of Wounding (regardless of what we call it) is that we eventually realize that acting from our Wall is a choice. Even though the events that caused us to build it were more often than not external and "not our fault," maintaining it is really our own doing.

Abuse Is Real, but Being a Victim Is a Choice

If you have been violated, attacked, hurt, or abused, the role of victim is real in the moment. No one should ever deny you that. Life is often unfair and cruel, but how you live with the emotion and energy of the attack is where choice begins. When staying in the mind-set of a victim is no longer necessary, you must find the will to see things differently and, as some people say, "reclaim your power." By this, I mean that you return to the energy of your essence and overcome your Wall that has cut you off from who you really are.

"No one can make you feel inferior without your consent."

— attributed to ELEANOR ROOSEVELT

Do we all really have a Wall of Wounding? It doesn't sound pretty, and for people who pride themselves on strength and perfection, it's just plain hard to admit. But, *yes,* we all have a Wall of Wounding. In fact, the sooner we can accept this as a universal experience and quality, the sooner we can do something about it. Much of this lives in what Carl Jung called "the shadow," the unexamined and denied places within. We all get hurt, we all react, and we all have tender places we don't like to go to. This is normal, and there's nothing to be ashamed of.

If you think about your own Wall of Wounding, you'll realize the millions of ways it can be built. Since it's made of the energy and emotion of *any* experience that rejects or doesn't affirm your essence, that means *anything* or *anyone* could build it up, depending on the situation: your parents, siblings, teachers, friends, neighbors, images on TV or in films, positive and negative experiences, well-intentioned people, and those who deliberately seek to hurt others.

It Could Happen Anywhere

A little girl looks at a magazine and sees manufactured images of tall, slender women or buxom beauties; and she begins to feel shame for her natural appearance, wondering if she could ever look like that. A boy loves to sing and dance but is ridiculed by his father for liking something that's "only for girls." A child learns best while moving or doodling—a tendency supported by research into learning styles by education psychologists— yet is punished by a teacher who expects her students to sit up straight at all times and be quiet. These are the moments when we build our Walls.

Even if your mom and dad seem "perfect," there can be a deep fear of failure and endless self-judgment rooted in your own Wall of Wounding. If parents don't take interest in the things that make up their child's essence, this may result in excessive guilt, shame, self-doubt, or even an incessant desire to please. Observing my own child, I have noticed how the "terrible twos" are a stage and process in which some of the Wall is formed through the frustration of being fully conscious and yet not fully in control. It must be a terrible time for the child, although Western cultures place more emphasis on the inconvenience to the parents who have to experience tantrums and excessive fussiness.

What Do I Have to Prove?

I was an undiagnosed dyslexic as a schoolboy, unconsciously inverting numbers and letters as I read. Certain subjects that used a lot of numerals, especially math and science, were painfully frustrating for me. Eventually, I just assumed that I was "stupid" in those areas. My spelling was also impacted, which made aspects of English class as well as other languages difficult. Fortunately, although I read very slowly, I still loved to read and write. In high school, that awful feeling of confusion led me to withdraw all effort from subjects that I perceived as threatening, such as algebra, chemistry, French, and physics. This fear of failure continued after I graduated and when I was in college, where I studied as hard as I could to overcompensate for my fear of proving myself inadequate.

What I didn't realize for a long time is that I was wrong. It took being a valedictorian on the dean's list during my honors B.A. studies as an undergrad, plus attaining a full academic scholarship for my M.A. and Ph.D., before I realized that I might be more than I had come to believe! Maybe I wasn't stupid after all.

My doctorate program with the Graduate Theological Foundation had a close affiliation with the University of Oxford in England. My advisor, the renowned scholar Ewert Cousins, had made the recommendation that I defend my dissertation before Oxford faculty. Only when on a plane to London as I studied my material with panic in my heart did I suddenly realize: *I've made it so far! What more do I need to do to prove that the beliefs I had about myself were false?!* What people saw on the outside was an accomplished scholar, always rising to the top of his class, but what I felt inside was fear that I would be revealed as "less" than others. Today, many of the clients I counsel who are high achievers are driven by a similar wound.

While there may be a soulful quality to the work and direction of your life, there can also be old energy driving you without your knowing. You become aware of this energy as more and more problems show up, or as you sense that you're losing your freedom and ability to make choices in life. You've come face-to-face with your Wall of Wounding. Will you remain stuck in old patterns of thought and behavior, or will you confront this emotional energy and heal it?

In the next chapter, we will take a look at other people's Walls and the ways in which they were able to break them down and rediscover their own authentic essence.

◦◦◉◦◦

CHAPTER SIX

Examples of the Wall of Wounding

"Only those who dare to fail greatly, can ever achieve greatly."

— ROBERT F. KENNEDY

What Does It Look Like?

Here are some real examples from my experiences working with people as I've helped them connect their moments of wounding to their present life circumstances. Although parts are written as personal testimonials, they're really my own rephrasing of notes I wrote while in session. To protect the privacy of my patients, all the names have been changed here (and everywhere else in the book, for that matter).

Sindee

Sindee was a stay-at-home mom who had become a chronic caregiver for everyone in her life, including her three children, husband, extended family, and friends.

The constant demands were depleting her, but she couldn't find the strength to say no.

After recognizing and exploring her Wall of Wounding, Sindee realized, "I understand now that as the oldest of five children with a mother who was always depressed, I *felt* that I had to take care of my mom and everyone else. My dad rewarded me for my work, and I think I came to *believe* that my worth lay in putting others first. The story of my life is that caregiving defines me, and without it, I must be worthless—since no one put me first when I was young. At some point, I convinced myself that if I didn't look after others, I would be abandoned and unloved."

Richard

Richard was an entrepreneur who went from one business scheme to another. Some worked out, but most failed, yet he was always chasing the next best thing. He dragged his family all over the country and was angry at all his missed opportunities. His relationships were failing, as was his health.

Richard finally realized that he'd hit a wall, explaining, "I've always been creative, and it truly is my passion to be a part of a new business. But what I now clearly see is that the relentless, often reckless, drive that went along with all this really originated in my youth. My dad, who grew up in a poor family, worked very hard for everything he had. He never paid much attention to my interest in sports or my more sensitive nature. Instead, he instilled a *fear* of poverty in me and the sense that I had to do better than he had to make the family proud. I *felt* that my worth was solely based on my financial success."

Gail

Gail's mother and father were both successful physicians, and she attended private schools from a young age. Although her family was deeply loving and always supportive, Gail's role models were high achievers, and she often felt that she could never quite reach her parents' high standards.

"My mom and dad were Mr. and Mrs. Perfect. I wanted their love and attention so much that I did everything I could to live up to their polished record, but it felt so impossible that I eventually gave up. At 16, I started doing drugs and abusing alcohol. I kept my dark side hidden well enough to get through school, a job, and even into a marriage. Now I am divorced, and the pain of admitting that I'm a failure has driven me deeply into my addiction. I feel trapped. I am unworthy as an addict, but when I'm sober, I'm afraid that I'll never live up to my parents' expectations. They know about my problems now, and I see how disappointed they are."

John

While I was doing some research on healing programs used in prisons, I met John, a 22-year-old Native American man. We started talking, and he shared this with me: "Until I joined the spiritual-healing program in this place, I thought that my only options were to be an angry drunk or a lazy drunk. But now that I've met the Native American healers and counselors here, I'm starting to wonder if I really have to have that future, or could I be like these sober, happy people. Why am I so angry at myself? Maybe all the things that have happened to me weren't my fault. Maybe when I get out of here, I can become any kind of person I choose. I didn't know that people like me have a choice—until now."

Rosa

Rosa was born and raised in a devout Catholic family. Her parents were loving, hardworking, and kind, but there were certain things that were difficult for her to talk about. When she was ten years old, Rosa was sexually assaulted by a relative who was looking after her and her brothers while her parents were away. Afterward, the relative told her that she'd better not tell anyone or her parents would be angry at the sin *she* had committed and she wouldn't go to heaven. Rosa lived with the guilt, shame, and loss of power for years. As a teenager, she developed problems with her weight and moods. She was depressed, and nurtured herself with food.

One day she decided to confess everything to her priest, thinking that he would keep her secret and that talking to him would be like talking to God. Sadly, the priest knew the relative she spoke of and assured Rosa that she was mistaken about the incident. He even scolded her for creating such a "teenage fantasy." It was the last time she ever went to church. Once she finished high school, she moved across the country to escape her family and the pain of her secret. She lost weight, took a job that paid the bills, and married the first man she ever dated. She liked the feeling of security and looked forward to not having to worry so much about dating or her appearance.

Before long, Rosa and her husband tried to have a child but weren't successful. Sex was uncomfortable and confusing for her, and soon her husband lost interest.

Rosa gained her weight back, and her husband criticized her for that, as well as her inability to conceive. She simply accepted that this was what she deserved. Rosa had felt worthless and powerless as a result of the abuse; she believed that her body was something to be ashamed of and that the world really wasn't interested in her fate. Years later, when her husband became more distant and was obviously having an affair, the pain of her life began to surpass the pain of her Wall of Wounding.

"At this point, I can see it all clearly, but up until now it has been impossible," she said. "I hated myself, and in a way, I hated my family for not knowing or sensing what had happened. But I was also too scared to ask for help. I've made all my decisions as an adult to avoid having to face and feel all the loss in youth—my family, my relatives, my sexuality, my self-esteem. I was so full of hurt. Being numb was the only way to survive . . . or so I thought.

"I see now that there is more to me than my suffering. I've met other women who have confronted their pasts and overcome their pain. I don't deserve to be treated badly by anyone, and I believe you when you say that I have an Essential Self inside, because that is what I feel. I know there's more to me than this pain—it's just a shell that started off as a scar and ended up as a mask. But it's not *me*."

Marco

Marco couldn't stay in a relationship for long. He was good-looking and charming but struggled to pay his bills or find meaningful work. He'd often become involved with someone, and just as they got serious, he'd start to panic and find a reason to end it. He was finally able to recognize his Wall of Wounding, and he wept when he realized all the people he'd hurt over the years.

"I remember Mrs. Bose, my second-grade teacher. It sounds so silly, but she was the world to me. My parents fought a lot, and my two sisters had created an alliance to support each other, but I was left out of everything. There was a big age difference between us as well. But Mrs. Bose was like my second mom. She promised that she'd always be there for me, and when I was in the third grade, I stayed in touch and saw her often during school hours. When I was in the fourth grade, though, Mrs. Bose got married and moved away. I felt totally worthless and unloved. I really had no one but her to nurture me.

"Now I realize that I've always been afraid that the women I care about will leave me. My family didn't seem to love me, and my second mom left me. I can see that my life revolves around this fear of being abandoned."

A Fence or a Cage?

More than stories of how we get hurt, these are accounts of how our emotions lie at the root of the mistaken identity that often follows. If we look at what limits our essence, we'll find a place of deep emotion. It rarely makes sense. The examples in this chapter are dramatic to illustrate a point, but simpler things can have huge impacts—an embarrassing moment on the playground, a misunderstood comment from a teacher, or a humiliation at a party, for example.

How it comes together is complex, but the Wall is the same for everyone. Remember that the Wall of Wounding is *the congestion of emotions and energies from experiences of disconnection that remain unaddressed, unexamined, or unresolved.* Imagine each negative situation or encounter as a pile of emotional bricks that we use to slowly build a wall around ourselves. We might also envision it as a dam, built one brick at a time to block the flow of the river of life. We hold back the energy of who we truly are, while placing our attention on the floodgates. Only *we* can control those gates; only *we* can decide who gets to experience the beautiful, natural flow of our soul.

In some ways, we create these barricades to protect ourselves. The Wall becomes a security system that lets us know when people, places, and things are getting too close to our fragile core or to mimicking experiences from the past that were uncomfortable or painful. The Wall is meant to prevent those things from recurring, but something happens along the way and the Wall works against us. Before we know it, we've cut off our *own* lives from that vital river of essence and energy, and we're on the outside of our own soul looking back in. It's a state-of-the-art security system *gone wrong*.

We've created a fortress with armed guards, barbed wire, and a secret code. The irony is that in securing our essence, we lock our awareness out! We become identified with our persona and forget how to get back in through the security system. Like a scene from an action thriller, one day we return to the Wall and ask the guards to let us in. Under strict orders to keep everyone out, they refuse to let us back in. We fail to recognize ourselves, so we have to look to the outside world to make sense of who we are. The fence that was designed to protect us becomes the cage that traps us in the persona. We're cut off from our authentic selves and from our Original Source of power, creativity, and joy.

Depending on history and experience, some people have massive Walls that are heavily secured, and others have thinner ones that seem less formidable. In certain areas of life, our Wall may be easily overcome, yet in other aspects, it may be terrifying to face. The Wall of Wounding, however, isn't the end of the story. It's what we do in reaction to it that leads us to where we are today. It's the *reaction* that is so complicated and difficult to undo.

That is the next step of understanding in this journey of self-discovery.

"I can guarantee you, just because you don't deal with something, that doesn't make it go away."

— JOYCE MEYER

◎◎◉◎◎

CHAPTER SEVEN

The Persona:
How We Get Lost Behind
Masks, Roles, and Expectations

*"Diseases of the soul are more dangerous
and more numerous than those of the body."*

— CICERO

The Persona Is Made Up of Stories

We've already come a long way, from the mysterious Original Source to our amazing Essential Self, and on to the unfortunate, although natural, Wall of Wounding. *What's next?*

For the majority of us, most of these aspects were shaped by the time we were teenagers. Developmental psychologists have long agreed that the first five to seven years of a child's life are the most emotionally formative. The traps of high stress, low energy, and bad habits may be rooted in the Wall of Wounding, but the real problems begin in the ways we adapt who we are in reaction to our experiences of disconnection and fear.

If you look back at the many examples of people's personal experiences—including mine—in the previous chapters, you'll not only notice the intense emotion and energy at work in their defining moments, but you will also note the many *stories* about self and life that were created *from* emotionally charged relationships or events. This process of reacting and creating stories in response to wounding is what I call "Persona building."

The Persona is the term I use for the face you show the world. It's the "you" created in reaction to life and not necessarily out of intention or essence. In other words, your Persona is hooked on what other people think and feel; it's who you think you have to be in order to make the world go around. The word *persona* just means "mask." Some people call this layer of the self the ego, but I think that word has been overused and misused. In addition, it becomes confusing because you have to sort out who is using it, how, and why. Remember that the *Persona is naturally your externally shaped self.*

When it's added to our evolving diagram, it looks like this:

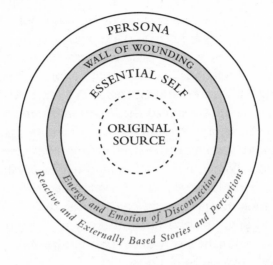

In a lot of modern healing work and self-help, people use the terms *stories, self-talk, scripts, internal dialogue,* and other expressions to refer to the worldview that the Persona is based on. I like the term *story,* for it implies meaning, complexity, and a sense of possible falseness. The Persona is the identity you create based on the stories you have observed, integrated, or rejected. It is fueled and motivated by the Wall of Wounding, and because of the Wall, it's cut off from the energy of the Essential Self. As a result, the Persona is not only built from the outside in; it's also shaped and fed from the outside.

Once any aspect of your life has been cut off from your essence, then you have also lost your natural connection to energy and vitality in that part of your life. When the power supply from the inexhaustible source of your Essential Self and Original Source has been cut off, where then do you get your power? If your work, health, or relationships are separated from their natural source of vitality, for example, how are they sustained? From the outside in.

Looking back at my experience with Marina and the pivotal moment when I observed and felt the pain in my parents' relationship, I saw that I adopted a story to go along with the emotional energy. No one forced it on me, and I could have read the situation differently. But I didn't. The story I created was that "men are the cruel brutes, and women are the kind victims. Men need to be overcome; women need to be supported. Men's anger is bad; women's emotions are to be attended to." In addition, I took on specific personal stories, such as "I'll be the good guy; I'll *never* hurt the women in my life." In some ways, I made a vow to be the opposite of my dad at whatever cost—even if it hurt me.

It's common to imprint either the same pattern of a parent or the polar opposite. We rarely land in the middle when it comes to reactions. Some people's stories are more blended or reflect other primary caregivers or influences. If you look at your life and your tendencies toward Inspiration Deficit Disorder, you'll likely find that you are either repeating a family pattern or acting in extreme rejection of it. In either case, it has shaped your Persona.

I could have come up with other stories or perhaps identified with my dad. I could have decided that anger gets you what you want—that anger wins. I could have determined that women are weak or that aggression is okay for men in relationships. I didn't come to those conclusions, but a slight shift in my personality, the timing, the culture, or the context and maybe I would have taken the story in an entirely different direction.

Oftentimes, you can look at a family and see common experiences yet radically different reactions. The Essential Self accounts for much of this, as do a thousand other factors. It isn't worth trying to solve *why* you picked up the exact story you did; you only need to recognize and understand *which* stories you adopted.

Changing Your Story Changes Your Life

When your story about how the world should work doesn't match the way it truly does work, that creates stress—plain and simple. Change your story in an empowering way to match the way the world actually is and in most cases, the stress will dissolve. So many spouses confide in me that they're waiting for their partner to be different, or people in business tell me that their co-workers should be acting or behaving in some other way.

I've also counseled parents who have shared that they "expected" their children to call home every other day once they moved out, and when they only got a weekly call, they were very hurt and confused. "What did we do wrong? She should call more often if she loves us!" I hear that quite often, but it's just a story. "She" calls according to her story, and even though it's just once a week, she still loves you!

Common Persona Stories That Contribute to Inspiration Deficit Disorder

There are lots of stories that add up to stress very quickly. Here are several examples:

- People should always be on time.
- Plans should be followed exactly.
- The more I do, the better of a person I am.
- If I don't fill my time, I am lazy.
- Self-help is for other people.
- Emotional language and expressing feelings is a sign of weakness.
- Nice guys finish last.
- Money is the answer to my problems.
- I always have trouble with money.
- I have to look after other people first.
- No one will look after me but me.
- You can't trust people.
- "They" are all alike.
- If I don't have a lot of money, I'm not successful.
- If I don't have a partner, I am not lovable or worthy.
- My husband should know what I need.
- My husband should [anything].
- My wife should understand me.
- My wife should [anything].
- If only my body were [fill in your wish].

Unless you've told someone your story and what you expect, it's foolish to assume that he or she will live up to it. Other people are living according to their own stories—not yours. Remember that when your story matches your experience, *stress will immediately be reduced.* If you haven't already, take the time to watch the film *You Can Heal Your Life,* which follows the life story of Louise Hay. It also features self-help experts discussing the role of our stories and attitudes in healing. It's an amazing resource. I own the DVD and have watched it many times—and I learn something every time. It has helped me, and many of my clients, develop a greater awareness of how we talk to ourselves.

Own Your Stories

As human beings, stories are how we move through life. Even the idea that we should live without stories is a story. What is most important is that we have a sense of mastery over them—that is, we need to know what they are and why we're choosing them. In Joan Borysenko's great book *It's Not the End of the World,* she talks about some compelling research on realists versus optimists. Time and time again, she illustrates, the realists fare better in coping with outcomes. This doesn't mean that we shouldn't aspire to something greater or have visions of a better way of being, though. Realistic optimists look for the positive in each situation with a sense of practicality that guides their level of expectation.

Practice becoming aware of when you get attached to a story and sense what you're *expecting* from your Persona's hungry emptiness. Instead of acting on impulses, take a deep breath and try to *feel the other possibility* in your essence. Make a soulful choice, and then let it all go. Trust and see; learn from what happens.

Watch Your Language

It's been interesting for me to see how many of the stories that are running people's lives are culture bound. If you visit a new place, you'll find new stories about how life *should* be. Cultures exist in cities, villages, countries, special-interest groups, communities; and among races, religions, and regions. There are many forms and sources of culture. These stories about love, work, health, family, and time clearly lead to a very different experience of the world. Pay attention to the language of other cultures and you'll learn a lot about their story of life.

Most Native American people, for example, traditionally have a story that viewed being a parent as a job to look after a "gift" from God. In other words, your children aren't really ever yours—they are God's. You are simply blessed to have the role of parent and the joy of loving your little ones. But how long your children live and how well they live is really between them and God. It's not about what you want. The possessive use of language (my son, our daughter) is about relationship, not ownership or control. This story makes for a different experience of parenting.

Another example of language shaping our stories can be seen in America today. Life is viewed by many as a war or violent struggle. It's embedded in our stories. We watch films of extreme violence and somehow see ourselves in the characters who have to kill to save the day. When we get upset, we say that we "blew up," and when we win, we say we "beat" the other person. We use expressions such as "I'm going to kill him," "You have to fight for your rights," "war on drugs," "war on terror," and the "battle against cancer." We worry that disappointments will "destroy us" or "be the end of us." This language sets up a fear-based, oppositional relationship to life.

Change your story, change your language . . . and you will change the way you experience the world and the way the world treats you.

I'm on a Roll—Watch Out!

Another way of being caught up in a story is to become overidentified with a role. Many people not only believe all the stories they've created or have been told about life, but they also turn those stories into roles. A role is like a job or a part in a play—it's a type of mask or label. We create a role when we turn what we do into who we are. We become our label. In my life, I *act* as a father, husband, son, brother, healer, author, boss, employee, nephew, relative, American resident, Canadian citizen, spiritual teacher, Ph.D., minister, and a man. I do all these things! I could say that I "am" every one of these, but really "I" am much bigger than what I do. These are just titles, descriptors, and functions I perform; they can change, and I know that even more is yet to come.

Even those who know me best don't completely know me. I play my roles because they honor my Essential Self and connect me to my Original Source, yet I'm always aware that there is more. I realize that I'm not a job or a title, nor can I be defined by my relationships. I remember the great mystery that I'm a part of; I remember my essence. I have yet to express who I fully know myself to be, and I have yet to know who I am fully capable of becoming.

Don't be defined by your roles. Someday your role will change: you may lose your job or retire; the kids will grow up and move away; and your looks may fade with time and so might your power, wealth, or influence. Poverty, illness, and poor health are also roles that individuals take on. You've probably heard things such as "People like me can't make that kind of money," or "People like me don't get opportunities like that." That is just the imposition of an old role. If you don't like it, change it. If you like it too much, let go of your attachment to it.

Revisiting Our Examples

If you look back at the examples in the previous chapter, you can see that the stories were created out of emotionally charged experiences. If you have a hard time figuring out your own stories, review the ones I provided in Chapter 6, and try to pick out the stories. Then take at look at my notes and compare what you discovered with what I've offered here.

— Notice how Sindee recognized that her helping was a result of her understandable impulse to contribute to the challenges of her home life growing up, and yet turned into a lifelong role. Fed by the fear of being rejected or unloved if she didn't fulfill her role, Sindee's story about caregiving ended up consuming her time and energy while hiding her true self. Her story dominated her choices and sense of self-worth.

— Richard, the entrepreneur, concluded that security would come through wealth; that his father's approval would only come if he were financially successful; and that he was basically unlovable without fulfilling those conclusions. That strong fear led to a life built on irrational ambitions, habits, and needs.

— Gail, the daughter of two high achievers, concluded that if she couldn't be perfect like her parents, then she was worthless, undeserving of even her own love. She also believed that numbing her pain was better than facing it, and that other people's approval was more important than her own Essential Self.

— John, the young Native American, felt his whole world was defined by what he had seen around him. Because he observed and experienced violence, he believed that brutality was an acceptable way to relate to the world. John even accepted shame and pain as natural feelings that he didn't bother to seek remedy from. His story considered those experiences normal.

— Rosa, the ex-Catholic and abuse survivor, moved away from home and into a miserable life. The sexual abuse she experienced as a child taught her that her body wasn't something to be proud of; rather, it was a source of hurt. She learned that family, religion, and men couldn't be trusted. Likewise, work was just a way to make a living, and marriage was just a way to hide from loneliness. Rosa fed the emptiness inside her with food and hid her emotions behind her weight. She carried a story that said that being attractive was dangerous, and her body remembered it.

— Marco, the man with relationship troubles, told himself a story that said loving leads to suffering and trusting leads to abandonment. His story said that as long as he didn't care about people too deeply, he wouldn't have to face loss or betrayal.

Each of these individuals experienced the world through the stories they had unconsciously and consciously accepted. They made choices and took actions to support, justify, and live from their stories each and every day—until they became aware of them and realized that their picture of the world was just a reaction to their own Wall of Wounding.

Looking at your own challenges or greatest opportunities, you might ask yourself what assumptions you're making about your limits. What about your potential? What do you believe about your ability to achieve your goals? Is there a story that *you* need to rewrite?

A Persona-Based Life

"Once you label me, you negate me."

— SØREN KIERKEGAARD

Having a Persona is neither good nor bad. If your Persona reflects your Essential Self, it could be a great thing, but if it overshadows your essence, it can be disastrous. Keep in mind that your Persona can contain any type of story, such as the following:

I expect myself to be . . .

- The fat one
- The thin one
- Angry
- Sad
- Poor
- Rich
- Sickly
- Never sick
- The clumsy one

- The helper
- The forgotten one
- The star
- The black sheep
- The activist
- The wild one
- The comedian
- The martyr
- The hard worker

Where did your story come from? Does it feel like a choice? Does your Persona reflect your soul? You'll know if your identity is essence based or Persona based, because a Persona-focused life or aspect of life has certain core qualities, such as the following:

Persona-Based, Reactionary Living (Inspiration Deficit)

- Reactive
- Controlling
- Overacts
- Underacts
- Compares
- Competes
- Overly focused on goals
- Overly active mind
- Worries
- Projects onto others
- Has lots of expectations
- Easily disappointed
- Easily stressed

- Codependent
- Addictive
- Compulsive
- Tends to be overly withdrawn or social
- Focused on what "should be"
- Takes things personally
- Has a hard time letting go
- Very critical
- Passive; avoiding
- Attacking
- Denial; resistant

These qualities aren't exhaustive, but they give you an idea of what to watch out for. These are simple indicators: when you experience those types of behaviors and feelings, you are in your Persona, cut off from your essential energy by your Wall. But remember this is also another way of saying that you're a normal human being!

You've probably noticed that many of the previous traits are opposites and don't go together. An attacking quality and a tendency to withdraw from situations are both examples of Persona-based actions and are prime conditions for Inspiration Deficit Disorder. What they all have in common is that they're conditional, reactive, and *based on the behaviors and actions of others.*

On the other hand, examine how life looks when you identify mostly with your Essential Self. These are the qualities that show up instead:

Inspired Living

- Makes decisions based on inspiration and essence
- Evaluates based on integrity
- Focuses on intent
- Heart-centered; balanced mind
- Trusts
- Takes ownership of choices and emotions
- Has few expectations
- Looks for the lesson
- Resilient
- Stress passes quickly

- Connected
- Maintains healthy personal boundaries
- Compassionate
- Consciously choosing
- Knows how to step back and evaluate
- Fully present
- Focused on what is
- Doesn't takes things personally
- Purposeful
- Releases; lets go easily

The Roots of Inspiration Deficit Disorder

The key difference between an inspired life (essence based) and a reactive one (Persona based) is the degree of inspiration present. Inspiration is the expression of the Essential Self and Original Source in daily life. When inspiration is a part of how you engage the world, then your attitude and experience shift to the qualities like those in the previous list. When inspiration is missing, however, you might be successful, but you'll never be satisfied for long. Your life might look good on paper or to your friends, but you'll always feel like something is missing.

This is where Inspiration Deficit Disorder begins: with the loss of the Essential Self. It's rarely something you consciously choose; and even when you make certain sacrifices in the name of family, income, career, or society, you almost never realize that it could cost you your health, happiness, vitality, and sense of purpose or meaning. Many paths of the Persona start off seeming like a great idea—a clear road to follow. This is natural because the Persona takes its cues from outside influences and disregards the soul.

Choices in schools, hobbies, relationships, religious involvement, diet, sports, fashion, social circles, home design, and personal expression are all easily co-opted by the strong voices of peers, family, ambition, and self-promotion. Everyday advertisements and commercials prey on people's inspiration deficit. Instead of saying, "Put this magazine down and go for a walk!" or "Turn this TV off and get a life!" they say, "Buy this!" "Listen to me!" or "Act now!" . . . happiness is just a click away. If only you buy this product, you'll finally feel complete.

Dr. Wayne Dyer, a legendary author and speaker, has written about this in his own way. Recently, he also starred in the film *The Shift,* which explores the Persona. I like the caution he presents, highlighting that most people today feel one or all of the following three things:

- *I am what I have.*
- *I am what I do.*
- *I am my reputation.*

Naturally, none of these things is true. They're just passing aspects of your life, a small part of who you really are.

Five Forces of the Persona: Beware!

The last thing I want to leave you with in this chapter is a very important note about the Persona. Somehow, it takes on a momentum and life of its own. Down the road, this will work in your favor, when you learn to align your Persona entirely with your essence. For now, this is something to be cautious of. *The momentum of the Persona is rooted in five natural forces.* Pay attention when they show up, as you can be pulled further and further away from your Essential Self.

The trickiest part about the forces of the Persona is that when you're unaware of the harm they can do to your health and happiness, you may actually embrace them, using them to justify why you are the way you are! These factors are intrinsic to Inspiration Deficit Disorder and will keep you stuck. As you'll see in the next chapter, the Persona gets hooked on patterns of energy and repeating cycles. It's self-perpetuating by design, so take note: it's *meant* to be hard to overcome.

The five forces of the Persona are:

1. Approval

2. Judgment

3. Denial

4. Blame

5. Rationalization

In my past work as a business consultant with IMPAQ (**www.impaqcorp.com**), a fantastic corporation based in Los Angeles, my mentor and boss, CEO Mark Samuel, showed me how, time and time again, these five behaviors were at work in the lives of dysfunctional managers, teams, employees, and even in the culture of larger organizations. I've observed that these factors go far beyond the workplace and are universal in those who have Inspiration Deficit Disorder.

If you can work to end or minimize all or any of these, you will have begun to undo the impact of Inspiration Deficit Disorder on your life. Until you minimize, manage, or dissolve these forces, an inspiration deficit is just a step away.

1. **Approval** is all about the attachment to positive feedback. It isn't just about wanting to do a good job; it's about seeking recognition, wanting to be praised, affirmed, or complimented in some way. These are all forms of emotional reward and can become the motivation for a huge range of behaviors, including ones that are unhealthy and even destructive. One of the biggest problems with approval seeking is that it often looks good on the outside, but there is a disconnect on the inside.

You may be liked and appreciated, but it's exhausting. If approval doesn't follow, then you'll often feel disappointed, hurt, angered, or rejected. True soul-centered behavior needs no approval or affirmation; it is self-sufficient.

2. **Judgment** is much more than just being critical. It's okay to be discerning and thoughtful, having a mind that can spot flaws. Judgment is an energy and an attitude. It holds an implied value system—that something must be bad or worse for something else to be good or best. Judgment carries a negative evaluation for anything that isn't in agreement. It's about looking for flaws and faults with an emotional evaluation attached.

Instead of saying, "This isn't my style," judgment says, "This is valueless," "This is wrong," or "This is stupid." It is oppositional and self-centered. Sadly, it feeds the Persona, and many people actually feel good when they judge others. Gossip, politics, religion, and social circles in most cultures today are overrun with judgment. Remember that it separates you from your essence.

3. **Denial** is one way to put off facing something. Other methods include procrastination, deliberation, avoidance, or a focus on judgment and blame. But it all adds up to denial. You are in denial when you fail to recognize or own a problem, limit, or difficult situation. Most people don't even consciously notice or acknowledge that a problem exists. I believe that nine out of ten times the awareness is close at hand; it's just that these individuals who are in denial never take the time to allow themselves to become aware of the situation. They keep themselves *distracted*. This is why many people rely on blame.

4. **Blame** is the act of placing the responsibility for the cause or solution to a problem on another person. Usually, it's about trying to make someone else the sole source of a situation or your behavior. You may say things like "I'd be happy if you didn't always . . . ," "I'll relax when they finally stop . . . ," or "I'll change when they finally admit that they. . . ." Blame can be fun, and it's easy to get other people involved. Turn on the TV and you'll see news show after news show featuring "professional blamers." These expert commentators are affiliated with one view or another and blame those who are unlike them for the world's problems. Modern American popular political commentary is mostly about blaming and rarely about resolution, compromise, or problem solving.

Some people actually look good when they blame because it sounds intelligent and thoughtful. The sad part is that they remain a part of the problem instead of the solution. Be careful as you look to transform your own life. The energy of blame will show up the moment things get difficult. It usually starts with: "It's not my fault," "I have to . . . ," or "I wouldn't have if only they didn't. . . ."

5. **Rationalization** means that you look for evidence to show that your fears, impulses, or habits are justified. When you rationalize, you use stories of the world and your own past to stay stuck. You might say, "Because my parents were mean to me, I don't understand kindness so I can't help being mean to you," or "I never had help. No one made it easy for me, so why should I help 'them'?" or "I can't help being abusive because I was abused." If you're looking for evidence to allow yourself

to stay the way you are, beware! The world is so wide and full that you can find evidence for anything. Do you want to prove that something is unfair, likely to get worse, or that you *have* to control or react? You'll find that evidence if you look hard enough. There are lots of people making poor choices, so you can easily find someone to reference.

Don't forget that you can also find evidence for the opposite: for the best possible outcome. Be optimistic; if you look for the lesson and opportunity, you'll find it. It's a matter of perception. As the author Richard Bach once stated, "Argue for your limitations, and sure enough, they're yours."

The Healing Power of Awareness

Sometimes, learning to observe, recognize, and label your patterns of thought and feelings will be enough to begin a radical unraveling of the ties that have kept you tangled. For most of us, the process happens slowly and with intention. You can dissolve the reaction-based Persona a little at a time; first by cultivating an ability to slow down whenever you feel old reactions, stories, and emotions taking hold of you. Then with some deep breaths and a conscious step back in your mind, just notice what you are thinking and feeling. Pay attention to what is going on in your body. Give yourself permission to have reactions and old habits. Take a moment to accept and forgive yourself, but then move your attention to your highest intentions and intuitions, and begin your next step from there.

Developing an ability to witness *and* experience your old emotions and stories is important. Ignoring them will not help, as they'll simply accumulate and wait for you deep in your mind, heart, and body. Every aspect of your life experience has an energetic dimension, meaning that thoughts and feelings are also "energies" that move through your body and interact with the world around you. Understanding the role of energy in the development of your identity, health, and process of transformation is key. Whether you come to view energy as a literal force, like electricity—as most spiritual traditions see it—or whether you see it as a metaphor, "energy" is a critical concept to understand in the process of awakening.

The next chapter will help you review the role of energy in Inspiration Deficit Disorder and assess the ways in which you manage your own levels.

Do you have an "energy crisis"?

⊚⊚◉⊚⊚

CHAPTER EIGHT

Your Identity Map: A Review of the Role of Energy

"The aim of life is to live, and to live means to be aware, joyously, drunkenly, serenely, divinely aware."

— HENRY MILLER

Are You Connected to Your Source Energy?

The next step in understanding Inspiration Deficit Disorder involves identifying how you use, waste, and manage your energy. This is a crucial element, so to make this clear, here's a concise review of our journey so far, which you may want to refer back to from time to time (it may be a good idea to bookmark this page).

As you read, you'll arrive at a definitive picture of how inspiration deficits set in, as well as the role of energy concerning your habits, addictions, and dependencies.

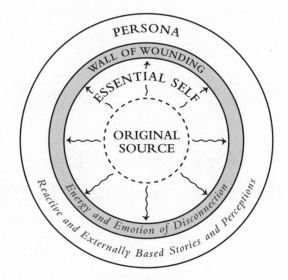

Note: Where the Persona reflects the Essential Self, energy flows.

— In the beginning, there was nothing but Source Energy, the energy of potential, intelligence, and life. There was nothing other than the energy of Love and Connection. This energy can be called Life, the Universe, God, Spirit, Consciousness, or any of a thousand other names—scientific, religious, and everything in between. This energy is the Original Source.

— The Original Source energy transformed into life as we know it and remains the essence and context of all things. Creation, destruction, mystery, and endless potential are all natural characteristics of the way this Original Source expresses itself.

— Source Energy is within you, and when you were born, it expressed itself (so to speak) through you. This unique matrix of talents, preferences, passions, energy, and purposes is your Essential Self.

— When you connect to your Essential Self by expressing it, being aware of it, and making decisions that honor it, the Original Source within you is activated and engaged. You experience it as vitality, joy, satisfaction, and balanced energy in your life.

— The hurts, wounds, disappointments, and experiences that disconnect you from your Essential Self also disconnect you from your vital source of energy by creating a wall between your awareness and your Essential Self.

— The energy and emotion of all your disconnecting experiences accumulates in a Wall of Wounding. This Wall insulates the Essential Self, in some ways protecting it, but mostly isolating it.

— Any childhood experiences that felt like fear, pain, and disconnection contributed to your Wall of Wounding. Major traumas and prolonged imbalances experienced during adulthood also add to the Wall.

— As your Wall of Wounding grows, your connection to the energy within diminishes.

— As your Wall of Wounding was formed, so too was your Persona—the collection of stories, attitudes, roles, expectations, and perspectives that you adopted in *reaction* to the world. The Persona is not typically your own intentional design. When you're separated from or not attuned with your essence, there are only two choices: reaffirm your Essential Self, or build a new external version of self in reaction (which is your Persona).

— The degree to which you are identified with your Persona is the degree to which you are cut off from the vitality of your Essential Self and Original Source. Having low energy, seeking adrenaline rushes, or being overly driven or stuck and unmotivated are all examples of what it feels like when the vital force is cut off from your life. This is the beginning of Inspiration Deficit Disorder.

— The degree to which you are cut off from the energy of your Essential Self is the degree to which you are likely to become *hooked* or *dependent* on the energy of the world around you. This shows up in the form of habits, addictions, dependencies, and unconscious behaviors. This is when Inspiration Deficit Disorder can become more serious and lead to debilitating emotional and physical health conditions over time.

— Your life runs on energy, like an engine or a computer. If you don't have enough fuel/power, your engine will eventually come to a halt. Energy can be attained sustainably from within (Essential Self) or from the outside (Persona), but at an unsustainable cost.

— Being attuned to your essence is so critical that even if you are physically healthy and financially secure, a total disconnection from your Essential Self will eventually come at a huge expense to your well-being, relationships, and sense of inner peace and contentment. This is why understanding the "energy" of life is imperative.

Going in Circles

Moving through these stages of development and energy is a perfectly natural process. It's how everyone is formed. The challenge, however, lies in whether you are shaped primarily by your Wall of Wounding or by your Essential Self. **The more that your life and the face you show the world is a reflection of your Wall (and not your essence), the more you will experience despair, disconnection, and distress. The more your Persona reflects your Essential Self, the more vitality and joy you will bring to everything you do.**

Examine the following diagrams. Remember that it's normal to move from one stage to the next. The most powerful way to maintain your connection to Self and Source is to re-create the cycle as often as possible. Re-cycle yourself! So this means that instead of life looking like this (stuck):

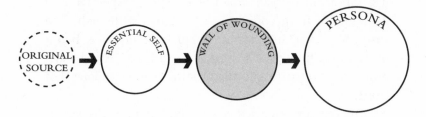

It would look more like this:

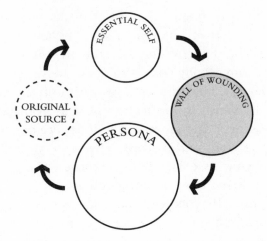

In the above figure, you can see that the Persona has been shaped by the Wall of Wounding, but then it returns to the Original Source for rest and restoration. It's important to take time out to gain perspective and detachment from your reactions. This can be achieved through prayer, meditation, a spiritual practice, being in nature, a hobby, or a sport, for example. (You'll learn more about returning to the Original Source in Part II of this book.)

Once you've stepped out of the habits of the Persona, then you can remember your Essential Self and your gifts, interests, sense of purpose, and what you truly want and need in life. From there, you acknowledge the wounded parts of yourself but are able to make healthier, wiser decisions, *building the Persona that reflects who you are and not what has been done to you.*

Being familiar with this circular flow will also help you understand the cycle of healing, which we'll discuss in Part II.

The Flow of Energy and Getting Stuck

Keep in mind that the place where you typically get stuck is in the Persona. As in the diagram that illustrates the cycle as a straight line, many people are solely shaped and influenced by outside forces, and that's when growing and learning stops. The energy soon dries up. In a life that is Persona based, you're cut off from the vital energy of your Self and Source, and there can be no real growth.

When you're separated from your natural life force, only one of two things will happen: you'll get sick, or you'll have to find alternative sources of energy. This is the beginning of habits, addictions, and negative or destructive thoughts and behaviors that often feel impossible to end.

Let's take a closer look at what it means to be "stuck" in the next chapter and explore specific examples and personal experiences.

⊚⊚◉⊚⊚

CHAPTER NINE

The Real Energy Crisis: How We Develop Habits, Addictions, and Dependencies

"As long as habit and routine dictate the pattern of living, new dimensions of the soul will not emerge."

— HENRY VAN DYKE

A Habit or an Addiction?

Lucy is a caregiver. It is her Persona—her role and personal story. Being a helper feeds her Essential Self, but at some point, she became filled with a constant need for approval and began disregarding or denying her own limits and boundaries. She put other people's well-being first, to a fault. When I met her, Lucy was more than just depressed and tired—she was physically ill. Some things feed the soul, some feed the Wall of hurt, and some feed both. Lucy's work and her role in her family was like that. Healing was what she was born to do, yet it was also slowly killing her.

Lucy got into health care because it was her passion. Helping others was her life purpose, and everyone knew it. If you needed support—emotional or physical—you'd call Lucy! As a child, she loved to play "doctor" and would bandage and tend to her stuffed animals. As an adult, Lucy became a registered nurse and served in some of the most challenging settings, including the ER, ICU, and the neonatal intensive care unit.

As I listened to Lucy's story, she spoke about her work with great fondness, yet I could clearly see the tiredness in her eyes. Finally, she admitted, "Somewhere along the line, things changed. I can't recall how or when it happened. I'd work long shifts at the hospital; and when I got home, I'd help the kids with homework, do the housework, and still find time to bake a pie for a friend's birthday or stop in to see if a sick neighbor was on the mend. People always told me to slow down, but that really didn't make sense to me. If I could do more, why should I take it easy? I wanted to be the best mother, wife, daughter, nurse, and friend I could be. That's who I was meant to be, I think."

Recognizing the heaviness in her heart and the low energy that hung like a cloud over her head, I asked what she meant by "I think." Lucy was silent. She looked down as tears welled up in her eyes and began to cry.

"I can't do it anymore. My husband was in a car accident last year, so he isn't able to work or help out much at home. My mom is in the early stages of Alzheimer's and lives alone, so I'm at her house constantly. My dad died five years ago. Work is also busy, and we're short staffed. I took some extra shifts, but everyone there seems so stressed-out and unhappy. I'm gaining too much weight, I don't sleep well, and I feel jittery. I feel like I can't settle down even though I'm exhausted. Is this what you mean by Inspiration Deficit Disorder?"

I smiled. "Yes, it's a bit of an advanced case. It's important to understand how serious this is. You can't go on like this—can you?" Tears still flowing, she shook her head.

"You know what, Lucy? It may feel like the weight of the world is pressing down on you, but think of it as a wake-up call. See it as a sign, a message that's as clear as can be, telling you that it's *time for change*. You *can* change all this. What if it were as straightforward as breaking a habit? Have you ever broken a habit before?"

"Oh, yes," Lucy said, rolling her eyes at the memory. "I used to smoke, drink too much coffee, and bite my nails. I've definitely broken a few bad habits over the years."

"Good," I replied, "because you still have a few you need to break. If you can do so, you'll be back on track faster than you can imagine."

Lucy started crying again. "You really believe that? I want to, but . . . it's so complicated. My sister was always the pretty one, my brother was always the smart one, and I was always the helper, the fixer. It's been like that since we were kids. I feel guilty about not doing enough for my mom, and I even resent my husband's injury although it wasn't his fault, of course. I'm so screwed up! This is going to take me years of therapy, and I just don't think I'll make it. I'm *so* tired."

"Lucy," I responded, "when a person loses her energy and inspiration, it's natural to feel the way you do. Your symptoms, your stress—it's *normal*. What I hear in the middle of it all is that once upon a time you knew yourself well and enjoyed a strong, energetic spirit. You created a good life out of your essence—by being true to who you are—and in many ways, your Persona reflects that. The trouble is that there are other aspects of your past, the parts that built your Wall of Wounding. There are a few "stories" that don't work. They have allowed your Essential Self to be overshadowed, corrupted, or go off track. What started as a good intention from your essence became a Persona, a role, which you struggled to sustain. You did it for others—not for yourself.

"You had the feeling that your parents admired your siblings because of their talents. You got used to being appreciated for how you helped out and not for exploring your dreams. This habit of helping also worked to fuel your Wall of Wounding. You had a lot working against your essence. The story you created says that it's wrong to say no to people, and from that you developed a habit of action: saying yes to everyone who needed help. You also cultivated a habit of thought: regarding your needs as less than others. And finally, you developed a habit of feeling: being worthy means that being uncared for and drained all the time is acceptable. But when you check in with your essence, your Essential Self, it's *not* okay, is it?"

"It's funny," Lucy replied, looking a bit brighter. "I guess I know what I need to do. I suppose I've always known when I got off track. I just didn't want to take action. I allowed myself to stay stuck because of old stories and strong feelings, but you're right. It's as simple as a new decision. Each day, each choice, should be one that feeds my soul."

"Yes, and you also need to understand something about energy and the Persona," I added earnestly. "It typically won't be an easy transition. Your Persona has been hooked, fed from the outside in. You've been connected to those external sources of self and energy for so long. No matter how much you want to end it, when you do, *you will feel resistance and discomfort.* Try to remember that's a good sign because it means you're unplugging from the dependence on what others think and are heading back into claiming your Original Source energy.

"Change sounds great, and it is. But on the way back into yourself, something will be waiting for you: the Wall you built so long ago. Those feelings will resurface, and when you attempt to put yourself first or try to choose differently, then guilt, shame, and hurt may show up. You'll hear the old voice saying, 'What if people don't like you?' 'It's selfish to put yourself first!' 'Maybe you'll find out that you're really not good enough after all.' You'll hear and feel those old beliefs, and then what will you do?"

"I don't know! What?!" Lucy looked panicked.

"Just keep going! If you know your choice is right in your heart of hearts, then just keep going. Get a support person involved: a friend, therapist, or family member. You are breaking an old habit, so it will take time. There will be reactions and discomfort, and you have to continue moving forward. Your brain needs time to relearn some things, your body needs to shake off some old energy, and the people around you may need some time to react. It's all fine. *Just keep going.*"

Lucy left with a written plan of what she was committed to doing differently and a list of timelines and specific people who could help keep her on track. The formula was simple: *concrete action steps, deadlines for each step, and a reliable support system.* Six months later, I got an e-mail from her saying that it was hard for her to believe it, but her old habits and routines were slowly changing, and she was regaining her health and peace of mind. On top of it all, because she committed six months to working on herself before trying to make any radical changes in her relationships, she found that the clarity and solutions she needed simply appeared—but not until she was firmly centered in her essence once again.

The Energy Hook

At the very core of any inspiration deficit is a cycle of behavior that feeds old and ineffective stories about life. I call this an "energy hook" and it is based on the Persona stories that were formed in *reaction* to the energy and emotion of wounding or disconnection. These stories when unconsciously chosen reflect your experiences, culture, and conditioning, as well as the role models in your life, such as your parents or other significant individuals; and they need to be fed.

Parents do play a key role in the shaping of those stories and the resulting behaviors that sustain them. As I've mentioned, the typical response to our parental experience is to either emulate or completely reject the behavior we witnessed. This means that your unconscious response will rarely be modest, thoughtful, or a meaningful balance of what you've experienced. When you're wounded, your reactions are often extreme. Later in life, you'll see that you are "just like" your mom or dad and feel trapped, or you'll realize that you've unknowingly sworn to never be like a certain parent and you're trapped by that expectation. Energy hooks are behaviors that have typically been modeled for you somewhere in your past, but not always.

Right or Wrong, a Hook Is a Hook

I call the behaviors that feed our stories and reactions energy hooks because they're self-perpetuating and keep us sucked in. Understanding why a behavior is a *hook* is critical. It explains why we get stuck in cycles, develop bad habits, and fall back into ineffective patterns when we're under stress.

To comprehend this, let's return to the story of your life so far and add an awareness of energy hooks:

- Your ultimate origin is the source of all interconnection, energy, and potential.

- Your potential, energy, and creative force are expressed through your unique essence.

- When you honor your essence, your own natural vitality springs forth. This is universal energy, which is limitless.

- Your Wall of Wounding and Persona are formed in any area of your life in which you experience *disconnection*—meaning that you become separated from your Essential Self and Original Source (which are your life force).

- Whenever you're living in your Persona, *you are cut off from your natural vitality.*

- **In response, you need to either change the situation, your attitude, and your behavior; or find a new external source of energy.**

- **An energy hook is any behavior that feeds you externally. It isn't about what you do, but why you do it. The motive is Persona based.**

- **Whenever you feel out of balance, you can be sure that an energy hook has taken over and is diminishing your energy.**

- *All external energy sources are unsustainable.* **They all decrease over time. Eventually, you'll look for a new one or experience the cost of the habit/hook.**

Was Lucy addicted to helping? Was she codependent? Maybe. I'd rather look at it in another way: Lucy was disconnected from the natural energy of her essence and instead reached out more and more for the energy she felt from the approval of others and from her role as "the helper." Nothing is wrong with this; however, relying solely on energy from the outside just isn't practical or sustainable.

You may enjoy being smart, pretty, athletic, or powerful, as well as being a problem solver, a member of a religious community, a parent, a spouse, or any number of things. When that lifestyle becomes a role that you have to serve—one you can't stop, step away from, or let go of without feeling lost—*then* it's a problem. That's when you know you have Inspiration Deficit Disorder.

More Examples of Energy Hooks

Maria Breaks the Habit of Self-Judgment

Maria went from one bad relationship to the next and landed in a marriage she thought was different from the others, until shortly after the honeymoon. Her husband always undermined her abilities—high demands, little praise, and always a critical eye. Over time, she just accepted his comments and her hurt feelings. On some level, she was repeating an old story. Accepting the insults was *energetically* fulfilling in a strange, unhealthy way. Eventually, it became a habit, and a vicious cycle followed.

Maria's husband was her primary relationship—this is where she sought approval and a sense of self. Since Maria was "just a wife" (in her words), the more her husband was unsatisfied, the harder she tried to please him, afraid of failing. The longer he stayed angry with her, the more evidence she had to rationalize that she deserved the poor treatment and bad feelings about herself.

When Maria's husband divorced her for another woman, she realized that it was a blessing in disguise. For the first time in 20 years, she was free to be herself. It wasn't difficult for her to think of at least a few things she'd want to explore or bring into her life. However, the problem that didn't go away with the divorce was the old habit of judging herself. Unintentionally, Maria once again carried her limiting beliefs and stories into her new life and found herself frustrated and unhappy again.

Eventually, she realized that "I don't deserve to be happy; I should expect the worst" was just a story she created in reaction to the hurt and disappointment in her life. All of her negative habits, such as always putting others first and not asking for what she needed, "fed" and energized that story. Maria reasoned that *if she pulled out the hooks that fed the old story,* then maybe it would fade away or change into something else. And that's exactly what happened.

When Maria stopped analyzing, judging, and doubting herself, her life began to change. When she stopped expecting the worst and started exhibiting a little bit of pride in herself, things began to transform even more. Maria learned to get her energy from within and let go of the need to define herself (bad or good) by her relationships. She used affirmations to help replace her old thought habits. Through sheer focus and will, she tried new things; and when her old stories and feelings showed up, she told herself: *I am worthy of more than this, and I deserve to be happy and healthy. The world needs me at my best!*

At first, she said this to herself all of the time: when she woke up, while she did a morning breathing exercise, before each meal, before bed, and every time she needed to replace a negative feeling during the day. As she became more aware of her essence and experienced new reactions in herself and from others, Maria began to feel and believe her affirmations. Her new choices changed her.

Denzel the Workaholic

Denzel worked from 7:30 A.M. to 8:00 P.M., Monday through Saturday. On Sunday, he tried to be present with his family and friends. If it weren't for the beer and football, though, nothing would slow his mind down. Denzel was successful in his career, but his health was slipping, as was his relationship with his wife and kids. He only had a few work friends and realized that he didn't have anyone he could confide in. His Inspiration Deficit Disorder was prominent, and he wanted out of his own life. The trap for Denzel was much like it is for most workaholics. He received a glimmer of satisfaction and a jolt of energy with each small success.

On the other hand, his successes never added up to a more meaningful life because they didn't honor his Essential Self. They had kept him hooked on working at his career compulsively for years. He also received a sense of pride and praise from his co-workers, many of whom either worked as much as he did or admired his "dedication." As it turns out, his dedication was really more of an addiction.

Denzel needed positive habits, people to support him, and a rigorous new schedule with a determination to stick to it. All of these steps are much like those used to treat alcohol and drug addiction. Together, he and I created a new plan: find alternate sources of energy, reveal and break the old roles and stories, and feed his true self. It started simply, but it dramatically changed his life.

First, Denzel spoke to his assistant and main co-workers, explaining that he had to make some changes for his health. He said it was "doctor's orders," which helped him feel justified in his needs. On Tuesday and Thursday, instead of going to work at 7:30, Denzel went to the gym first. On Wednesday night, he went to a yoga class on the way home (his idea). He still started work at 7:30 on Monday, Wednesday, and Friday; but he left the office every day at 6 (instead of 8) and decided to check only his phone messages on Saturday—no e-mails. Sunday was 100 percent off-limits for work except for emergencies; otherwise, no contact whatsoever.

In addition, Denzel committed to at least one date with his wife a month, one walk with her a week, and more time with his kids. His plan wasn't about changing the world, becoming enlightened, or training for a triathlon. Rather, it was about breaking old habits, setting positive new ones, and reconnecting with his essence. Once he got through that first stage, things really took off for him.

Karen Expected Too Little from Her Relationships

Karen unknowingly carried the burden of her father's mistreatment of her mother. Her dad was handsome, charming, and a superstar at work; but he treated his wife poorly and put little energy into his marriage. Years later, Karen found herself in the habit of having boyfriends who were good-looking but who didn't share her interests. She didn't realize it, but she expected very little of men, and a sense of despair grew in her over time. She thought she could be fed by a false sense of love and looks alone. Her alcoholism grew out of the emptiness she felt at a dead-end job and the old story that "real men" don't talk about their feelings and can't be expected to bring much to a relationship. On some level, she never expected to be truly happy, yet was frustrated that she wasn't.

Karen decided to stop dating for six months and found a healthier way to connect with people and feel appreciated by volunteering at a youth home. She also started to see a therapist. Soon she discovered things about herself that had nothing to do with her history and everything to do with her natural talents and needs. She realized that she could feed those needs by engaging with and giving back to her community. Her drinking problem resolved itself, and after her dating hiatus, Karen met an amazing partner who was also volunteering at the youth home. He treated her like a queen, and although she was uncomfortable at first, she decided to let him!

Rob Can't Let Go of the Past

The wounds from Rob's past were deep. He had been driven into his work by a desire to please his demanding father. He had grown up in poverty and wanted to prove that he could rise above it. He was also unpopular in school and was determined to overcome his sense of rejection by being the star of every team he played on.

Rob was a top performer in everyone's eyes, and that's what he needed in order to ease his self-doubts. However, while he was overly focused on the past, he'd forgotten the "team" that was his family and the witness that was his Essential Self. When Rob reorganized his priorities and became fed from the inside out, his life changed forever.

Joe's Anger

Joe's anger was aimed at himself, and he was trapped. His own insecurities were draining him and made him frustrated and short-tempered. Each time he got mad at someone, he felt a release from his own inner struggle and a little more in control of his world. At the same time, he also felt worse because he knew that his raw, misguided outbursts were hurting others. It was an endless cycle—the anger served as both his solution and source of pain.

Like the work and relationships of many people, Joe's anger fed and drained him at the same time. Recognizing this aspect, however, is the first step to overcoming debilitating stories and making positive changes.

Eric's Use of Pornography

Eric's addiction to Internet pornography was more about finding a secret way to exercise control in his life. The feeling of searching for more pleasing images and getting away with it was a source of peace for him. He felt powerless in his father-in-law's business, and his wife was often controlling and critical. His use of pornographic images was an escape that meant little about his respect for women or himself. Eric eventually sought help because he knew that his compulsion didn't seem "right," but he felt lost without it. It provided him with an energy source, yet he was running out of steam at the same time.

What Feeds You?

Everyone needs to be fed in one way or another. Although we don't use the language of "energy" much in the Western world today, we all know what it means to be "fed" by our work or relationships and to be "drained" by them. We speak about things "not being the right fit" or "being fulfilling," yet those are really metaphors for the energy exchange at the heart of our lives. Few choices are ever neutral. They either support our intentions and highest good . . . or not.

Watch how the energy flows in your life. Is it from a cycle, a habit, and something that you must have in order to feel okay? Or does it flow freely from your essence? Examine each area of your life and ask yourself whether or not you feel inspired.

In the following figure, you can actually see the way in which energy hooks draw vitality from the outside in. Unlike soulful choices and relationships that pull energy from your unlimited Original Source, the Persona requires external validation, distraction, and power. And unlike the energy that comes from your Original Source, energy hooks aren't sustainable. They become loops, cycles, or habits because a single taste is never enough. A dose of approval or energy from the outside is short-lived and requires you to constantly return to the people, places, and things you're dependent upon.

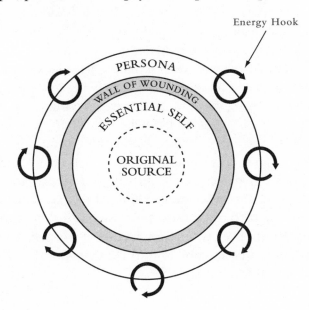

It's All about Energy

If your life isn't inspired in one way or another, if you aren't living from the inside out, then you will naturally reach out to external sources of energy. These come in various forms. External energy sources are essentially any behavior that results in an affirmation of the Persona or

Wall of Wounding. Think of someone who gets a "rush" from engaging in unhealthy or risky behaviors. We also use the expression (although not very polite) that a certain friend "gets off" on winning, helping, being a victim, fighting, or being stuck. It's hard to see it in yourself, but it's not uncommon to look at other people's behavior and sense that their motive may not be aligned with their essence. Oftentimes, you can see when an energy of imbalance is at work. Inspiration Deficit Disorder isn't hard to spot if you know what to look for. Like many professional healers, I can usually see or feel an inspiration deficit in the physical presence of a person.

Sometimes you can actually perceive a person's energy that's "reaching" out to you. You feel this presence like a vacuum, as if it were trying to suck out your energy. These individuals can drain you. Other people have energy that is "retreating"—you sense that they aren't totally present, and their eyes have a faraway look. You may feel like it's difficult to really get to know them. On the other hand, centered people, those who are living with inspiration, possess a bright, yet calming, disposition. Even when they're tired or stressed, you can still sense a basic stability to their energy or the "vibes" you pick up from them.

Inspiration Deficit Disorder and the Pursuit of Excellence

A significant portion of this book deals with strong examples that often highlight lifestyles and experiences that are not ideal, but it's important to note that Inspiration Deficit Disorder is also an issue for people who are healthy and flourishing. In fact, it's incredibly common among those who are successful—even those who are soulfully successful. There is no specific "type" of person who's more prone to an inspiration deficit—everyone is at risk. This may be the number one universal condition in the United States today, possibly in the world. Living out of balance is an illness that healers, saints, and sages have diagnosed and been treating for centuries.

Shakespeare wrote about it, Jesus preached about it, the Buddha taught the ancient art of overcoming it, and shamans tell the same story: *Live your true self or die by your falseness.* It's all about integrity and honoring what makes you absolutely unique.

Many highly successful people are that way because they honor their Essential Self. In time, however, and with the powerful influence of family, peers, society, and the Wall of Wounding, their gift can become a role, a mask. Sometimes we discover a hidden motive behind our drive to succeed. Many Hollywood celebrities fall prey to this phenomenon. Fame and popularity corrupt their capacity to stay true to themselves. A reckless life-style; wild drug abuse; and bizarre, offensive behavior are often just indicators of individuals' desperate reach for new energy sources. Because their energy hooks are failing and they're cut off from their own essence, they reach out for whatever will feed or numb them.

Another way in which Inspiration Deficit Disorder shows up in soulfully successful people has to do with time and change. What was once the calling of a person's essence might not always be. For example, I've known many Fortune 500 CEOs who have made an incredible mark on the world and achieved their dreams only to discover one day that it's no longer enough, or it's not right anymore. These people are faced with change, the next act. Even the most inspired executive, musician, actor, yoga teacher, minister, psychologist, customer-service clerk, football player, parent, piano teacher, or waiter must confront the challenges of changing interests and tastes.

Looking at these situations from an energy perspective, we can see what a difficult position it could be to get caught in. It often sounds like this: "I love what I've been doing, but I feel like I'm done. I still keep doing it because I don't know what's next or how to stop! I'm the one everyone looks to for inspiration, but I'm starting to feel stuck myself. It's getting harder to do what I've always done effortlessly. It's as if my energy is dropping. It looks good on the outside, but something isn't right."

I've seen many wise and wonderful people develop Inspiration Deficit Disorder simply because they didn't know how to leave something when its time was up. The Essential Self has endless depth. New frontiers of talent and service always lay waiting to be revealed. Sometimes the next stage of life is a more spiritual one, sometimes it's more about service to the world, and sometimes it's about self-care and family. Even the most enlightened masters may not know what is next or what the force of Spirit has "planned" for them.

Realize that it's okay not to know. It is okay to test and try different things—to develop new interests and hobbies while you are still in or are ending old patterns and careers. Start to explore what you love. Taste it, try it, and when you find what connects you to your essence, your energy will soar again. As you will soon learn, the level of your vitality will always help keep you on track. The solutions in the second Part of this book are as much for people struggling as they are for those who are ready for the next amazing stage of their lives.

The Deepest Intention: The Greatest Power You Can Express

Ultimately, everyone will encounter difficult choices when seeking healing and balance. There will come a time when you will manage your Wall of Wounding, your Persona, and your energy hooks well enough to live from your essence. Although life won't be perfect or without difficult times and emotions, vitality, joy, and purpose will become your foundation. You will know that you're living with integrity and fulfilling your Essential Self. It's a nice place to get to. It is, however, not a resting place; once you find balance, the greatest opportunity of life has only just begun.

Once you've embraced your Essential Self, the next challenge is to step aside and allow the Original Source to freely, spontaneously, and intuitively express itself through you. Ideas of "manifesting," "attracting what you want," and creating a life that matches your soul become secondary to trusting in life's process and the wisdom of your Essential Self. Opening your heart and mind to a deeper kind of wisdom and grace will work through you if you allow it. It becomes more and more about surrender, and not personal will or desire. Some refer to it as "letting go and letting God."

The Good News about Extreme Inspiration Deficit Disorder

What happens when everything we were taught doesn't work or make us happy anymore? In contrast to the previous section on successful people with Inspiration Deficit Disorder and the magical depths that await them, many of us consider that stage of life to be more of a fantasy. Some people are at a point where almost all hope is lost—when the silver cord of light that connects us to our Essence is so stretched it feels as if it will break or has already dissolved. In such moments, our Persona runs our life, and we no longer see the edges of its vast reach. We move from one energy hook to another, and our life feels as if it were spiraling out of control. Somewhere in the middle of the storm, the small, faint voice of our Essential Self screams out for help, just before we crash and burn.

In the addictions world, this is called "hitting rock bottom." In the medical world, I have seen people whose Inspiration Deficit Disorder has gone so far and for so long that it results in chronic health conditions that are untreatable or with emotional/mental-health problems that have no biological basis. Often it comes with one final event that "pushes you over the edge." It could be one decision to drink, become violent, isolate, self-harm, or escape that is so dramatic that the cost and chaos become unavoidable.

In my work, I do everything I can to help people who have inspiration deficits avoid this extreme place because the cost can frequently be steep. The damage to self, health, and relationships can take a great deal of time to heal. An extreme case ensures chronic stress that is crippling. There is substantial research showing that stress is the number one leading factor in causing or aggravating nearly *all* the dominant illnesses or conditions in society today! If Inspiration Deficit Disorder is the primary, universal source of this stress, then eradicating it means avoiding disaster.

The Gift of "Rock Bottom"

Remarkably, even in the face of risk, illness, and lost love, the momentum of a life out of balance is just too much to overcome before disaster hits. Sometimes, rock bottom is unavoidable. The miracle of the human design, however, is that a total breakdown is one of the most powerful ways to awaken to the Essential Self. It's difficult to imagine, but colliding with the extremes of Inspiration Deficit Disorder is often the best place a person can reach. Why? Because rock bottom occurs when all the energy hooks have run dry and all the Persona stories have failed. There is nothing left behind the wounds *except* the Essential Self. This is right where we want to be to begin the process of transformation from within.

Many of my clients have proven this to me, but Jenna's story expresses it best. Her parents were refugees from Southeast Asia. Accomplished professionals (a university professor and a physician), they were humiliated and driven from their beloved homeland, fearing for their lives. Many of their family members went missing or were unjustly imprisoned. Cut down and defeated in their prime, they fled to America, only to find themselves in an unfamiliar place that was hard on foreigners who didn't speak the language. All of their training and experience went unacknowledged, and they were forced to start over. They taught themselves English; had a daughter, Jenna; and spent the rest of their lives running a gas station.

Jenna's Wall of Wounding was full of pain, hurt, guilt, shame, and lots of confusion. Her Persona stories were shaped in part by her bitter parents, who wanted to provide her with the best of everything but really couldn't give her much. They were both depressed, harsh, and demanding. As a result, Jenna escaped her unhappy family life as a teenager in order to find her own way.

Street-smart and naturally talented, she was 16 when she left home and found her way into a youth program that helped her finish high school and then go on to complete a bachelor's degree in business. Through her hard work and pursuit of an internship opportunity, Jenna received a placement at a large information-technology firm, where she quickly shot up the ranks due to her obsessive drive to work hard and be the best. When I met her, she was a high-paid project director in her midtwenties. She was also a complete nervous wreck and a recovering addict.

After working day and night almost every day of the year for three years and medicating herself with cocaine and alcohol, Jenna hit rock bottom. "One night," she confessed, as a tear ran down her face, "I found myself in my office. It was around 11 P.M. on a Saturday. I hadn't eaten properly for weeks, I was pushing too many projects, and I was busy working with international clients at all hours. I realized that I couldn't remember the last time I genuinely laughed or hugged someone, and gave up the idea of having a real friend or boyfriend. I looked out at the city from my office window and *wished* that I could jump out. I even tried to open it, but no luck.

"I felt desperate and searched my purse for cocaine so I could numb the pain, but I had spent all my money on my last 'hit' (which I had done earlier that afternoon *in my office*). I went to the executive boardroom where I knew we had a stash of booze for special clients and special occasions. I picked up a bottle of the hardest thing I could find and went back to my office. Then I drank until I passed out.

"I woke up on the floor of my office on Sunday afternoon. Immediately, I was violently ill, and it felt like the world was slipping away. I had this vague sense that some of my co-workers had probably come in that day, passed by my locked door, and knew that something was wrong. It occurred to me that they probably had figured that out a long time ago.

"For a moment, I felt overwhelming shame and hopelessness. The pain of how awful and hollow my life had become was overbearing. I just didn't want to live anymore. I wished I'd died that night. Everything was wrong and broken."

The room was heavy with the energy of Jenna's story, but I wasn't disturbed. She spoke with a quality of indifference and clarity that led me to wonder what was next.

"Then," she went on, "it hit me. Like lightning. Like a sunrise. Like I woke up for the first time. I didn't need to kill myself because I realized *I was already dead*. No one really knew me. My soul had been lost to work long ago, I had no friends, and my parents hadn't heard from me in years. Even if I really did die, the only thing people would have said is that my life had been a sad waste. They wouldn't have said things like 'I wish she worked harder,' or 'I wish she was more popular or prettier.' It would have been more like 'Too bad she wasn't happier, too bad she didn't look after herself, too bad so much talent went to waste.'

"What I realized in that moment was that as long as I was living a false, uninspired life, I wasn't really living. And if I wasn't really living, then *I had nothing else to lose*. All those bad habits and addictions aren't who I am—so why should I care if I give them up? Those roles and expectations at work—they aren't me either, so why would I hang on to them?

"I felt like I was given a second chance that day.

"The next day, on Monday, I handed in a request to go on vacation immediately; I had seven weeks saved up that I had never taken. I told my boss that I also needed an additional few weeks after that. Then I did something totally crazy.

"I had always wanted to go to South America to work with the rehabilitation of jungle animals. I know it sounds odd, but I've always been fascinated and drawn to this topic. I uncovered a passion for the animals that are hurt by logging, hunting, and people trying to poach and export them abroad as pets. So I went online, looked up a volunteer program, and left a week later. I was gone for four weeks! I met amazing people, and even laughed for the first time in years. I fell in love with the rain forest and all the creatures there—birds, snakes, jaguars, dolphins . . . and I *will* go back!

"I'm taking time to regain my health, and I'm also applying to veterinary school. That is what I've longed to do all my life. I love animals, and I want to help. I want my life to matter, and I just can't make decisions because of people (or to spite them) anymore."

Jenna's excitement settled, and she looked down at the floor thoughtfully. "You know," she continued, "I think that following my dreams *is* what will make my parents proud. To do what they couldn't and to do it well. And if they don't like my choices, well, as long as they are my best and most fulfilling choices, then I can live with them not loving my job. Who knows, maybe they'll love me anyway, but what I've finally realized is most important is that I know *I* will love me."

It has been years since I counseled Jenna, but the last e-mail I received from her included pictures of her at an animal sanctuary in South America. She was in her second year of vet school. She looked radiant, too. Happy, healthy, and having the time of her life.

"Although the world is full of suffering,
it is full also of the overcoming of it."

— HELEN KELLER

◎◎◉◎◎

PART II

THE INSPIRED-LIVING PRESCRIPTION: HOW TO CREATE LASTING PEACE, VITALITY, AND JOY

"A journey of a thousand miles begins with a single step."

— LAO-TZU

Part II Overview:
Walking the Path to Inspired Living

For the remainder of this book, the focus is on solutions: *doing what works.* Now that you've completed Part I and have a clearer awareness of where you are and how you got there, let's turn our attention to the opportunity that life has presented you with: the chance to change, create, and inspire.

If you've jumped to this section, I would like to caution you. If you don't understand the roots of Inspiration Deficit Disorder and the map of how you grow (and get stuck) that is outlined in Part I, all of your good efforts and intentions to apply the teachings in Part II to your everyday experiences can fall apart. There are forces greater than your mind at work in your life. Your history, emotions, and energy, as well as the Laws of Nature and Spirit, are all essential components to the symphony of your most inspired life.

The important thing to know about the final six chapters of this book is that they're about *action*. It's not enough to just think about these things. You have to get up and do these steps and solutions. Change and healing is always possible; but you must have willingness, motivation, and focus as part of the equation. You may need to borrow some energy from a friend, support group, or therapist to face the aspects of your life you desire to transform; and that's okay.

Keep in mind the vast perspective of Chapter 2: you are part of an infinite universe of potential. Billions of people have walked the earth before you and have met and overcome greater puzzles and problems than you can imagine. Whether you want to reach a higher level of success, end an addiction, avoid feeling stuck, or tame your distracted mind, you can do so if you try. Even the highest aspirations for enlightenment and healing the world are never out of reach. It all begins with a step.

Be honest with yourself as you build your plan for transformation, and if you need to, discuss your doubts with a friend who knows you well; or talk to a healer, therapist, physician, or life coach.

You are also welcome to connect with the resources, experts, and a range of extra tools and support featured on my Website. I'm happy to help. I've also developed a workbook to complement this book. It's a simple, personal journal to assist you in taking the ideas and action steps you read here and applying them to your life. (For more information, please visit my Website: **www.jonathanellerby.com**.)

Since this section is all about taking action and mastering change, here's a quick overview of some key ideas to keep in mind as you read.

The Four Qualities of an Inspired Person

Not every decision you make will be perfect as you implement changes, and not every situation will go as you'd like it to. So remember that *how you do things* is as important as *what you do.* You'll learn that *clarity, integrity, courage,* and *compassion* are the key qualities that a truly inspired person brings to every situation, relationship, and choice.

The Four Ways Your Essence Speaks

At the heart of effecting positive change is the manner in which we make decisions and our ability to know our Essential Self. Many people think they can't always trust or "hear" what their essence is saying, or they feel cut off from it. What most don't realize is that our essence never stops communicating with us, nor does it stop offering us guidance. We just forget how to listen.

You'll learn the ways in which *intuition, vitality, love,* and *connection* are ever present in your life and how they will guide your decisions and help keep you attuned with your authentic self.

Ten Steps and Ten Traps

Looking back through many years' worth of stories about the men and women I've watched shift from being "stuck" to feeling free, from habit to choice, and from disconnection to inspiration, very clear themes have stood out as to what works. You'll learn the ten most common, effective, and essential steps to creating an inspired life. Work through each one of these steps and you'll experience amazing changes. You'll also learn the most common mistakes in judgment as well as the pitfalls along the way. Although it's beneficial to learn from your own experience, it's also nice (and helpful) to learn from the experiences of others. Pay close attention to the traps!

Seek Out Help and Support

You aren't meant to walk this journey alone, nor are you supposed to manage all your changes by yourself. Let's face it: although you got yourself to where you are, why not draw from someone else's wisdom, energy, love, or counsel to get you to the next step? There is no shame in asking for help. You'll find some great tips about the kinds of support you might need and how to best use them.

Physical Considerations

Finally—and this is quite important—you cannot forget that your health, physical settings, and many other concrete factors shape your mood, energy, potential, and capacity to change. We will review the things you need to know about optimal well-being, prevention, and self-care to ensure that your inspired life is more than fantasies and wishful thinking. An inspired life impacts every aspect of self and health. How you eat, sleep, exercise, and relate to your surroundings are significant factors to monitor and address.

◦ ◎ ◉

Now that you've uncovered the map of your inner landscape and know that the "medicine" you need is already within you, are you ready to start creating a life of lasting peace, vitality, and joy? Let's get to work!

◦◎◉◎◦

CHAPTER TEN

Transformation from Within: The Two Directions of Change

"The secret of health for both mind and body is not to mourn for the past, nor to worry about the future, nor to anticipate troubles, but to live the present moment wisely and earnestly."

— THE BUDDHA

Cutting Inspiration Deficits Out at the Root

You've already read a lot of stories about other people's lives and the realizations and actions that have allowed them to make positive changes. These accounts speak to the common experiences and challenges that everyone faces. Even though we'd love to separate ourselves from those who are wounded, there is no line we can draw between the people who are "damaged" and the rest of us. It's all "us."

I've mentioned this previously, but I'd like to re-iterate the fact because it's important: to protect the privacy of the individuals and families I've met and counseled over the years, descriptive details and names in this book have been changed; moreover, a few stories represent a combination of people who've had similar experiences. Overall, every one of these stories is true and more common than you might imagine. They represent the lives of your friends, parents, siblings, lovers, co-workers, and neighbors . . . and even those you might call your enemies.

The question isn't whether you are the same, better, or worse off than the individuals featured here, but how well you can learn from what they went through. Do you see the interplay between the Essential Self, Wall of Wounding, and Persona in these examples? By examining someone else's energy hooks, can you now pick out and end your own?

Be a researcher of life! These are your case studies, and each one teaches you about human potential and the power of change. The more you can think in these terms, the more you can glean a fresh perspective into your own situation and make different choices. If you've tried to apply the lessons from the previous chapters to your own life, then you should already be well on your way to a deeper understanding of yourself, and that is key. Remember that the end of Inspiration Deficit Disorder begins with self-awareness.

Waking Up to the Truth

Without a doubt, awareness is the foundation of inspired living. Most people in the stories in this book didn't realize there was something wrong until a specific event or incident took place that made them aware of what they were doing. Unfortunately, the majority of us don't know that we have Inspiration Deficit Disorder until the symptoms become exaggerated. I can still hear the exasperated comments of past clients as they began to wake up to their inspiration deficits.

Perhaps you can relate to one (or more) of the following statements. What they have in common is that they all indicate that it's time for inspired change:

- "I don't like who I've become."

- "I've forgotten how to have fun."

- "I used to have so much passion and so many interests, but now I feel like I don't know myself."

- "How did I get here? I don't remember when my life changed—one minute we were married, bought a house, and had kids; then the stress got to us, and I can't believe the awful things I've endured for the past 20 years! I've been numb, but now I'm angry. How did this happen?"

- "Now that I'm retiring, I feel like I'm about to lose my identity. Who will I be when my work is done?"

- "I've always been a soulful person, but my life isn't working anymore. I'm not used to feeling lost. How do I know what's next?"

- "It started out as something I did for fun, but then it gradually took over all of my time and energy. I got into this job because I loved it, and now it's killing me."

- "I can't remember the last time I felt really happy. Life is just so busy. I used to exercise regularly, socialize, and love learning new things. What happened?"

- "At first, there was so much excitement as I built my business—one success came after another.

> Life just kept speeding up, and so did I. I felt
> invincible. Somewhere along the way, though,
> I started to become more controlling, more
> demanding, and less fun. People used to like
> me, but now they're intimidated by me. There's
> a hole inside of me, and no amount of money
> or praise can fill it. I didn't see this coming, but
> what am I supposed to do now?!"

Another commonality among these statements is that these people are certain that they don't want to be where they are. They *know* they're off track, disconnected from their essence. Always be good to yourself and remember that becoming aware *is* a big step. It takes honesty, humility, and integrity to admit that you may have made mistakes or that your life isn't what it could have been.

For many, admitting imperfection and moving past denial, blame, and rationalization feels like a sign of weakness. *It's not.* Embracing vulnerability and personal faults actually indicates true inner strength. Not owning up to missed opportunities is a defense function of the Persona and Wall of Wounding. In other words, it's just a way to stay stuck.

Two Ways to Heal: Inside Out and Outside In

Once you're aware of your need and desire for change, there are two key ways to address Inspiration Deficit Disorder: from the inside out and from the outside in. In reviewing the most powerful models and stories of healing, it's clear that both approaches are necessary and can even work together. However, transformation must always begin from within. Once that's achieved, it can be complemented by doing work from the outside in. Here's a visual representation of the processes as applied to our diagram of the self:

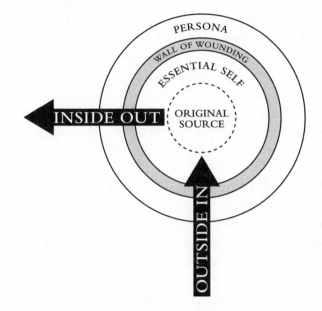

Inside-Out Healing

Healing from the inside out is self-directed and involves your relationship with intangible things such as meaning, purpose, and The Sacred. It involves intuition, diverse experiences, creativity, deep feelings, and an awareness of your energy. It's about integrity, your essence, vitality, love, and connection. Inside-out healing includes a great range of spiritual and energy-based healing techniques, including healing touch (energy work), ceremony, wilderness retreats, expressive arts, and shamanic journeywork. Healing from within is always possible; it's the antidote to Inspiration Deficit Disorder.

Outside-In Healing

Seeking change from the outside in means relying on the expertise of others—that is, your healing is in the hands of another person's knowledge and influence. Outside-in approaches dominate mainstream Western medicine; they are the techniques and remedies that typically involve a strong focus on the body or aspects of the mind, such as thought patterns. Both can be evaluated by professionals. On the other hand, healing from the inside out involves answers that only you know; it is based on your own capacity to initiate healing.

Outside-in healing might include treating your physical self with the help of medical doctors, as well as through diet, exercise, and detoxification programs. It could also include examining your mind and emotional state from the vantage point of the Persona. You might see a psychologist or counselor of some kind and explore the *story* of your past, your wounding, your family of origin, and your habits or addictions. There tends to be an emphasis on *talk*. Most of the dominant models of therapy today have this kind of focus. "Cognitive behavioral" therapy is a classic outside-in approach, although it's often modified by practitioners to incorporate other elements.

Not One or the Other

As magical and ideal as healing from the inside-out sounds, it's important to know that neither approach is complete without the other. This is where a lot of people get lost. For example, they might pursue medical answers to their poor sleep habits and high anxiety when the problem is a life of imbalance and reliance on energy hooks. Or they might be in therapy for years and learn to talk and think about their wounds and history but never really move past their painful feelings and into an inspired life.

The same issue can arise by using a strictly metaphysical course of action. I've met many spiritual seekers who think that their beliefs and rituals are enough to heal everything, and they refuse to seek medical attention or admit they may need a therapist. There are many people on the road to spiritual awakening who never reach the heights of enlightenment they seek because they don't realize that they're still in need of deep healing. The sad part for such people is that neither healing nor inner peace is achieved because the process is incomplete.

Oneness Is the One Exception

The only radical exception to this rule lies deeper than Persona and soul. Direct and overwhelming experiences of the Divine—the Original Source, the Spirit in the center of self—can be immediately healing and transformative. These are known as epiphanies, mystical encounters, "Aha!" moments, and even altered states of consciousness. In just a matter of hours or minutes, direct contact with the ultimate nature of reality can change your life forever. Now you can see why earlier in this book the very first step in the process to understanding your life journey was to discuss your mysterious origin: the radical love, interconnection, and potential that all things come from.

Knowing what this means as an idea isn't the same as a firsthand encounter of full-blown immersion and total ego dissolution. Although many scholars and spiritual seekers resist the idea, there *are* degrees or levels of spiritual experience. Everyone is capable of experiencing The Sacred. In its higher form, these moments involve being self-aware while *actually experiencing* the Persona, Wall, and Essential Self *dissolve* from awareness and *fade into* the vastness of the Original Source. This is what is meant by Oneness—the experience of all things as one thing.

Thich Nhat Hanh describes the concept well in his book *Zen Keys*. Other good examples of experiences of Oneness and their impact can be found in my own book *Return to The Sacred,* as well as in the following fascinating works: *Explorers of the Infinite* by Maria Coffey; *Healing States: A Journey into the World of Spiritual Healing and Shamanism* by Alberto Villoldo, Ph.D., and Stanley Krippner, Ph.D.; *The Disappearance of the Universe* by Gary Renard; and *Recovering the Soul* by Larry Dossey, M.D. I also recommend the audio recordings by author/ teacher Ram Dass, particularly *Cultivating the Heart of Compassion.*

Lasting Change

It's clear that healing from the inside out *and* outside in are both necessary and work together. Most people discover inside-out healing when outside-in approaches come up short or don't seem to deliver lasting change. The context and broader healing mission a person holds sets the stage for how the components of the process come together. When someone's approach to transformation begins with the outside world and then moves inward, the pieces of the puzzle don't always match up or create a clear picture. There is the energy of Persona and disconnection in the process.

However, when your life changes are rooted in the Essential Self and inside-out approach to wellness, then the outside-in practices, professionals, and choices can operate within an integrating and self-affirming vision. The next chapter stresses the importance of beginning all changes from within. When a change originates in your essence, then that change will affirm your vitality, resiliency, and joy.

◎◎◉◎◎

CHAPTER ELEVEN

Healing from the Inside Out: Living from Your Essence

"Follow your bliss."

— JOSEPH CAMPBELL

When the End Is the Beginning

When Marilyn came to see me, she was at a loss for answers. She was always feeling low, stuck, and depressed. The little spare time she had was spent in and out of hospitals, as doctors tried to diagnose a strange chronic condition she struggled with. They were calling it multiple sclerosis, but none of the interventions or therapies was having the slightest impact. Moreover, other symptoms would show up, such as migraines and arthritic pain, which caused some to wonder if it was really MS.

Not being a medical doctor, I asked Marilyn to tell me about her "inner life": how she used her time, what brought her joy, and the status of her relationship with her husband and children. She broke down and cried at these simple questions. Her marriage had felt loveless for more than 20 years, and her children had long since moved out of the house and were out of touch for the most part. Marilyn's attempts to stay connected with her kids were met coldly. She felt that most of her "friends" were really people who leaned on her for advice about their own miserable lives. Looking after all her friends and relatives, she admitted, left her no time to pursue hobbies or personal pleasures.

I decided to press the issue regarding her relationship with her spouse and friends, for these were naturally her two easiest opportunities for change. What I learned was disturbing. Marilyn's husband had been physically abusive to her in the early days of their marriage. As a new wife and mother of two toddlers, she didn't want to "give up" on her vows or look like a failure to her family. Over time as her children grew up, her husband ceased being violent and became more emotionally abusive. Whenever he was at home, he was either "buzzed" on alcohol or entertaining colleagues. It turned out that Marilyn's friends were mostly the wives of his business partners, and only one of them was someone she actually enjoyed spending time with.

Marilyn found our session difficult. We talked about how cut off she had become from her essence and vitality and that she would need to remedy that if anything was going to change. As we continued to talk, she opened up and shared more of her story.

Marilyn's husband never visited her during her hospital stays. Even when she was feeling extremely ill or debilitated, he still demanded that she host parties for his friends and keep up with the housework. He had outright refused couples' counseling and blamed her for all their marital troubles. The insults were daily occurrences, and there had been no physical affection in more than ten years.

Although I do *not* endorse or recommend divorce as a general philosophy, in this case, it seemed like an important step to consider. Taking into account Marilyn's medical condition, it was my belief that it might be a matter of life and death. She and I agreed that she would take all the steps she could to become a happier, healthier person; but if that still didn't make a difference, and if her husband was unwilling to change or heal as a couple, then divorce was a real possibility.

A Starving Soul Will Eat Itself

"Your soul is starving, Marilyn," I explained. "All the vital force you need, all the joy and direction you seek, you have it—you never lost it. But you have to start making your life reflect who you really are. You need to be certain that everything and everyone in your life feels like a choice, a *soul-affirming choice.*"

Marilyn started crying again, saying, "But that would mean I'd have to leave my husband! Everyone would ridicule me. I'd be on my own—I don't have anyone."

"Who do you have now?" I asked. "Let's make a list of all the people you don't want to lose—the ones whose opinions really matter. Then we'll build a strategy from there."

Marilyn's list consisted of her two children and the one friend she actually liked. She realized that she was as alone now as she'd ever been. She also saw that feeling alone *with people* who make unreasonable demands was probably more painful than being alone *without people*.

Dare to Dream

Marilyn and I talked about what it might be like for her to be on her own, focusing on her physical health and all the things that interested her. We discussed numerous ways she could positively change her lifestyle. In just one hour, we came up with a plan that felt simple, challenging, and yet possible. Marilyn's Essential Self seemed to be suggesting a short list of major changes. There were other factors as well, but these were key:

1. Improving her diet

2. Walking daily when she was physically able

3. Taking a painting class once a week at the community center

4. Listening to self-help audio programs (she liked Louise Hay and Joan Borysenko)

5. Investing in weekly sessions with a counselor for a minimum of six weeks

6. Divorcing, or separating from, her husband if there were no improvements after two months (usually I suggest a longer wait, but not in this case)

I also challenged her to a seventh step. Marilyn told me that she had originally wanted to be a schoolteacher for young children. She loved to help kids learn. So I asked her to add a "challenge step" and volunteer at her local children's hospital and read to the patients there. That made her smile, but she still asked, "Do you really think they'd want me? I'm a mess." I suggested that she offer her help and let them decide.

After writing down her seven soul steps, I asked Marilyn to make me three promises:

1. Act as soon and as quickly as possible on all these commitments.

2. Tell her friend what she was doing, and ask for emotional support and encouragement.

3. Talk with her counselor or doctor about how to make each of these changes safely, including assessing if her husband would be threatening or violent.

After that, Marilyn left my office. I assumed that I wouldn't hear from her again, since I met her while she was traveling on a vacation.

One year later, however, she came back to see me. I almost didn't recognize her. The deep lines in her pale face were gone. She was no longer hunched over and had put on some healthy weight. She smiled brightly when we greeted each other, and then she softly began to cry.

"It's me!" she exclaimed, wiping her tears. "I mean this time, it's *really* me. I have my life back, and I came to tell you all about it."

Marilyn was one of those rare individuals who heard the call of her Essential Self and finally, after years of ignoring it, listened and acted. She explained that as soon as she had gone home after her appointment with me, she told her husband they needed to talk. She confronted him about their past and said there was nothing left to save in the relationship. I didn't expect her to jump ahead on this step. He was shocked and angry, and tried to blame her. Then he accused her of spying on him, and it was revealed that he'd been having an affair.

Marilyn demanded a fair settlement and quick divorce. Perhaps out of guilt and shame, or maybe trying to keep her from embarrassing him, her husband settled their financial affairs quickly. She moved into an apartment in what she called a "fun, artsy" part of town and immediately began taking daily walks in the park for as long or as briefly as her health would allow. She also enrolled in a weekly art class, which soon led to a two-night-a-week commitment. Marilyn met new people in the class and embraced an entirely new social circle.

A New Life

As her health and energy improved, Marilyn also accepted the challenge of volunteering at a nearby children's hospital. She ended up falling in love with the unit of nurses and children she was assigned to. Her eyes sparkled as she recounted stories of the families she'd met and the profound ways in which her life had been touched by their love and hope.

There were many amazing details, and a few things caught me by surprise. Three months after she separated from her husband, Marilyn's children resurfaced in her life. Her daughter confessed that she'd been ashamed of the relationship that her parents had created and feared that she would end up like her mom. She also resented her mother for being "weak" and accepting such poor treatment. However, the change finally gave her hope and the opportunity to express her deep, undying love for her mom. Marilyn wept as she told me all this.

Looking at the glow in her face and her more substantial form, I had to ask about her health. "I guess you suspected it," she replied. "I guess I knew it, too: I'm better now. *All better.* No symptoms! No MS, no pain, no migraines. Yes, I'm doing my part by eating better, sleeping better, moving every day, and all that; but really, I think I was 'soul sick.' The doctors swear that my transformation is due to a healthy diet and exercise and perhaps misdiagnosis on their part. I don't know if anything they did ever helped, but now I'm better. And I know it's because I learned to love myself and feed my soul. I'm truly happy for the first time in over 20 years!"

The amazing thing about the inner self is just how simple it is to access its power. It's not always *easy,* and maybe not everyone can make dramatic changes the way Marilyn did. Maybe not everyone's situation is so cut-and-dried. After all, health isn't always so simple, and neither are relationships. Yet there is a timeless truth in her story that's relevant for everyone. It boils down to four things: clarity, integrity, courage, and compassion. To pursue these is to begin the path of inspired living and access your greatest vitality. Marilyn did it one step at a time; it wasn't easy for her, but her transformation was astounding. The process itself, however, was simple.

The Four Traits of an Inspired Life

1. Clarity

Clarity is about how well you manage your energy and intention. Stay focused and clear in your intent in every situation, whenever possible. Clarity is also about moving beyond confusion through understanding, communication, decision making, and the willingness to let go. You'll almost always be better off by making a small bad choice rather than staying stuck in your own uncertainty and the bad choice you already know. A step in any direction will give you feedback. Remember that no movement means no feedback!

Sometimes in order to gain awareness, action is required, even if it means that you just need to let go and accept things as they are. Always work toward being clear about your intentions, your commitment level, and your soul's wisdom and desires. This will improve how you communicate with others and how you feel about yourself. When you're focused and self-assured, you'll worry less, too. Achieve clarity and trust the process. Revisit your intentions for health, life, relationships, or whatever you're transforming as often as possible. You will be clearer by being intention based, and not reaction based in your communication and decisions.

2. Integrity

Living with integrity means that what you feel and know on the inside matches what you say and do on the outside. Integrity is *alignment*. It's not about adhering to an external set of standards regarding morality or good behavior. This is a self-referenced, soul-centered quality. It also represents ownership and responsibility. Integrity means your intentions are reflected in your conduct and mind-set.

It's vital to recognize your role in the situations you're involved in and remain engaged and responsive. You exhibit integrity when you honor your innermost self and live according to your highest truth—not according to the reactions and judgments of others. This may sound simple, but in reality, this is often difficult to maintain. Your integrity is revealed when you live with honesty, respect, willingness, and an endless commitment to revealing your Essential Self. You're living from a centered self—not being self-centered. You can ask yourself in any situation: *Do my actions reflect my truest intent and heartfelt values?*

3. Courage

Courage is one of the more underrated and underemphasized qualities in the lives of those with Inspiration Deficit Disorder. More often than not, the main difference between a person with an inspiration deficit and someone without one is whether or not you have the courage to act on what you feel and know in your essence. Think of it this way: integrity would remain just a good idea without courage.

Many things can test your integrity, such as peer pressure, society norms, and family values, but none of these can change who you are. In other words, if you feel a calling to do something differently but are afraid you won't be accepted, then you simply need to trust and do what you know in your heart is right. Keep in mind that your Wall of Wounding will make sure that if you wait until you *feel* like making a change, you never will. Your energy hooks will make sure that if you wait for an *easy* time to make a change, it will never come. And your Persona will make sure that if you wait for all the "right" *reasons* to change, they will never present themselves.

Courage is like a muscle: the more you use it, the stronger it gets. Trusting, releasing control, staying present, and being kind all take a powerful resolve in the face of old habits and patterns. Remember that *fear* is the most fundamental root behind all inspiration deficits.

The soul cannot blossom or be fully expressed wherever fear is allowed to grow.

4. Compassion

Compassion is something we all feel but have a difficult time expressing in words. Genuine compassion is about empowering ourselves and others while embodying kindness. It's about seeking the highest good in every situation, but *not* always trying to make people happy or "fix" things.

Compassion is being creative, always approaching situations with respect and a desire to understand. By doing so, you can overcome obstacles or hardships through patience, forgiveness, and taking a stand when necessary. You can be steadfast when it comes to protecting yourself or your beliefs, while also honoring your connection to all people and things. Maintain balance, healthy limits, and self-care, as well as the awareness that helping from your Persona rather than your essence isn't really helping at all. Remember that compassion is love in action—it's big enough to overcome anything. Sometimes it requires radical action, and other times restraint. To truly embody it is to embrace self-love. Master that and the loving-kindness you offer to the world will be limitless.

Fearless Living

All the stories of triumph in this book are about individuals who embodied the four qualities of inspired living according to their own understanding, but to the fullest degree. The measure of a man or woman lies in the depth to which he or she can live these qualities.

Gandhi was one of the greatest examples of someone who achieved this because he was a man of both peace and action. Some associate the qualities of the soul with weakness or passivity, but this couldn't be further from the truth.

You can learn to apply these principles to any situation in your life. For example, if you have a relationship challenge: (1) Get clarity on what you're feeling and how it translates into what you know, what you don't know, and what you need. (2) Communicate with integrity, which means to act and speak in a way that expresses what you feel and reflects what you hope to achieve. (3) Be strong and courageous. Don't let your discomfort or fear of not being heard or validated stop you from maintaining your integrity and being supportive of yourself and the other person. (4) Be kind and loving to yourself and the other person. Stay focused on the highest good and bringing out the best in each other. Stay away from blaming and judgement.

As you apply these principles in your life, you'll experience greater peace and less stress. This isn't just about being nicer to others; it's about being good to yourself as well. You'll feel empowered by your choices and more satisfied by the way you engage in situations. A soulful life is not a passive life, nor is it one of people pleasing or letting others take advantage of you. It's quite the opposite.

The Inspired One: A True Warrior

Through my travels and studies, I was amazed to learn that in many Indigenous and Eastern cultures, the greatest warriors were also the most devoted spiritual students. The qualities of the "wisdom keepers" were sought by warriors, for they knew that these sages possessed tremendous self-mastery, endurance, and discipline. Having mastered their mind and emotions, the "Inspired Ones" weren't reactive; on the contrary, they were clear and decisive, knowing precisely when to fight or withdraw. They understood the role of Persona and the endless cycles of energy hooks. Incredibly, at the root of these spiritual warriors' practice was an emphasis *away* from violence and the unnecessary use of force. Genuine strength was illustrated by an individual's ability to overcome provocation, and instead maintain composure and discernment.

Among the Lakota Sioux and other Native American traditions was the unexpected practice of "counting coupe." During battles, the greatest display of power was riding alongside or running right up to an enemy and rather than attacking, the warrior would simply touch his foe with a harmless "coupe stick." This act signified that the warrior had the ability to take a life and yet the personal will and restraint not to. It was an exhibition of mastery of the body and mind. Out of gratitude, humility, and respect, the defeated opponent would withdraw.

Build a Strong Foundation

The four aspects that make up the foundation of inspired living are also the main qualities of great parents, leaders, partners, and friends. They are the essential characteristics that will carry you into an inspired life. However, they can be misused if applied to old stories of the Persona and energy hooks. Creating a strong foundation fuels your awareness of your essence. This is the single most important key to ending Inspiration Deficit Disorder: *listening to your Essential Self.*

How the Soul Speaks

The day I married Monica was extraordinary. Our wedding reflected the many cultures of our families and the spiritual paths that have touched our lives. Most of the people we loved dearly were present. The ceremony was held outside, overlooking my wife's beautiful homeland: the piñon, sagebrush, and pine-covered mountains of Santa Fe, New Mexico. Despite the surrounding beauty though, it was difficult for anyone to get a good photograph. It was my fault, but I can explain. . . .

During the service, I found myself bursting into tears—repeatedly. Half of our wedding pictures are of me, red faced and tear stained, overflowing with love and joy. Unfortunately, when frozen by the camera, it looks like I was being tortured. The crowd shots look much the same. It seemed that I created a chain reaction of weeping that moved throughout the small crowd gathered. It was a good problem to have.

Why do we cry when we're happy? Why do we cry when we see other people's tears of joy? Why do things like love, passion, art, rock concerts, greeting-card commercials, and nature move us to such strong emotions? It's not that we're sad—rather, it's the soul responding to another soul . . . essence to essence. Because our essence is more energy and spirit than intellect and brains, it expresses itself through emotions. There is a force, or power, that is present when people engage their Essential Self. It's magical. When I'm in the presence of this living soul-force, it brings me to tears. Sometimes it fills me with excitement and energy. The expression of our authentic self is one of the world's most powerful forces, and we're drawn to it every day.

It's All Around Us

We can turn to modern television for some simple examples. For instance, *The Oprah Winfrey Show* is an international phenomenon. For some "followers," it's more like a religion. The stage is the church, and Oprah is the radiant minister calling her flock to awareness. Some disagree with her politics, others don't care for her fame, but everyone considers her a powerful woman. Why is this so? The bigger question, however, should be: "Why is Oprah as powerful as popes and politicians?"

I think it has to do with the truth—it's all about soul-force. The one thing that most of her listeners and viewers say is that they love Oprah because she reveals what is *real*. She questions and explores what she finds interesting or doesn't understand. She exposes the struggles and triumphs of the world while she stands in the center of her talents—her soul-force—and isn't ashamed to show it. That's true power. That is having a presence that shines for the entire world to see, and when people feel it, they want to be near it.

I also think there's a lot more to it than that. The *Oprah* show is also about showing life both as it is and as it could be. We're allowed to feel that it's okay to be "normal," and it's also possible to be extraordinary. She showcases people who *know* their true selves. They know their essence and aren't afraid to live from it. She also explores the horrid truth about what happens when we disconnect from our essence. This is her secret. Like her or not, Oprah is a soul revealer.

Although it may seem strange to offer examples from television, I'd like to mention two other great examples to consider: shows about singing and dancing.

Yes, reality shows! Why is *American Idol* so popular? Sure, there's the guessing game, loving and hating the judges, and the hook of hoping your favorite wins. That's all part of it. But I—someone who generally avoids the show and chokes at the commercialism—become engrossed whenever I watch. Why? Because among the yahoos and wannabes gracing the stage, there are the others who bless the viewers with a glimpse of being fully alive in their essence. When that moment hits, you get chills or a lump in your throat and feel a sense of awe as you're captivated by the raw talent exposed.

The same thing happens for many people when watching others dance. The television programs like *So You Think You Can Dance* follow in the footsteps of many talent, competition-style shows, which are ultimately about showcasing people who have learned to express their essence. In the dance shows, we see that it's almost impossible to *just* be a strong technical dancer and still be considered talented. The honesty of the body and surrender of the Persona are necessary for a radiant performance. Your body will always reveal how you relate to your essence. This is why in my book *Return to The Sacred,* there's a whole chapter dedicated to the ways in which movement—such as contemplative walking, yoga, and dance—can induce a spiritual experience.

I use television shows as my examples only because a lot of people today watch a lot of TV. Remember that this isn't the only way to see someone living his or her essence. I'm moved by the essence of life all the time—nature, animals, people helping each other, men and women standing up against the odds, children, my child . . . the world is filled with truth and beauty. Keats once wrote: "'Beauty is truth, truth [is] beauty,'—that is all / Ye know on earth, and all ye need to know." The Essential Self is always speaking to us; the trick is to learn its language and to take the time to listen.

The Four Voices of Your Essential Self

Once people understand Inspiration Deficit Disorder, one of the more common questions is: "How do I know what my soul wants? If I've been disconnected from my essence for so long, how do I begin to feed it and make decisions with it in mind again?"

Fortunately, the Essential Self never goes away, and it never stops speaking to us. It does get covered up, and we can get out of practice with it, like a language we once studied years ago but rarely use. The wisdom and clarity of our essence is always waiting to be expressed. In fact, the Essential Self expresses itself in hundreds of ways and in every facet of life. From simple things such as taste in clothing and music, to the hobbies, foods, people, jobs, and pets that attract us, the soul is always being revealed.

There are four dominant ways in which the Essential Self will let you know whether a situation or choice is in agreement with it: intuition, vitality, love, and connection. To know what your essence wants, you simply need to listen closely; then start trying things out and paying attention to the response you feel inside. Mentally, emotionally, physically, or spirituality, you *will* get an answer.

1. Intuition:
How Your Essence Speaks to Your Mind

Intuition is more than the accumulation of old information in an instantaneous brain blast. It's the gut feeling, the hunch, or "knowing" that defies experience or understanding. We've all had these experiences at one time or another. Some dismiss them and some, like me, rely on them for the most important decisions in life. Research has shown that intuition, understood or not, is a vital quality of a successful person in any field.

Mothers say that "a mom just knows," business people call it "acumen," and medical doctors consider it "good judgment." Often, it is nothing more than the small voice inside that gives us a clear sense of direction or action. Although we can't explain its origin, some part of us knows that it's correct. Following our intuition is critical in ending Inspiration Deficit Disorder.

So listen to your gut! When you make a decision, pay attention to the way your inner voice affirms or cautions you. Few people regret following their intuition. Most people's inspiration deficits reflect a pattern of ignoring their deepest sense of what is best for them.

2. Vitality:
How Your Essence Speaks to Your Body

Have you ever been involved in a cause you were passionate about? Have you ever loved something or someone so much that you were able to tap into an "energy" that allowed you to work extra hard, stay up extra late, or apply yourself more fully than you'd ever thought possible? Parents, entrepreneurs, performers, rescue workers, and artists do it all the time. When what you're doing is directly affirming or expressing your Essential Self, your vitality will increase. Quite literally, you'll have more energy.

Pay attention to when your choices raise your energy and excitement, as well as when they leave you feeling drained. Over time, you'll notice the difference between vital energy and attraction/addiction energy. What you get from an energy hook (such as the thrill of doing something well that isn't really consistent with your integrity) is more unstable in nature—that is, it feels more like an unsettled, "high-pitched" kind of energy. It's short-lived. Imagine it being like a jarring cell-phone ring or the buzz from a highly caffeinated energy drink. The soul's vitality, on the other hand, feels sustainable, reliable, and grounded. It's more like the way you feel after a good long rest or like the deep rhythms of the ocean waves—strong and steady. Take time to examine your energy levels.

3. Love:
How Your Essence Speaks to Your Heart

In any moment, you can always ask yourself, *What is in the highest good?* or *What would be most loving and empowering?* Despite your wounds and habits, you know what kindness is. Holding a door for someone whose hands are full, picking up a pen that someone drops, or being forgiving with a customer-service attendant when addressing a failed product that they personally didn't design—these are all easy examples of the ways most people know to be "nice." Nice seems simple, but it lives on the same spectrum as love and compassion. When you *feel love,* you act out of compassion with respect, gratitude, accountability, and kindness. When you commit a loving act, you are in your Essential Self.

The energy and mind-set of love will always move you into your center and reconnect you with your essence.

Things that create a loving feeling do the same, which is why daily gratitude exercises, volunteering, and falling in love are all experiences that somehow make the world feel like a better place. It isn't because of what other people are doing; it's because of the *feeling* of love inside you. Being in nature, with a friend, or with a pet are simple ways to create a loving feeling. All these things move you into your essence.

Don't be trapped by thinking that you have to make people happy in order to express kindness. Love is not conditional. Love and compassion are expressions of your essence, and they draw their energy naturally from your Original Source. True love is never depleted; it's a willing choice. Unlike the earlier notes about learning to *act* with compassion, in this case it is the *feeling* of love that indicates that the Essential Self is engaged. Notice whenever you feel it and what creates a loving feeling in you.

4. Connection:
How Your Essence Speaks to Your Soul

Think of a time when you experienced a "felt sense" of relationship to the world around you. You might call the feeling *interconnection* or *connectedness*. Maybe you were playing a sport, enjoying art, or taking a walk in nature, or perhaps it happened while giving birth or making love. It feels like the immediate personal awareness of the interrelationship of life. It's a moment in which more than thinking, you *feel* that you are a thread in the tapestry of creation and that every action you take ripples throughout the universe. In those moments, you know that nature, humanity, and all of the past and future are somehow connected. Perhaps it was a feeling of Oneness.

Such powerful moments are rare for some, and then there are the fortunate ones who come to those experiences with ease. When you encounter them, you're immediately reconnected with your essence, even the Original Source. Choices, worries, fears, and regrets fall away. In a moment of feeling "connected," the wisdom of your Essential Self is easily reached, allowing trust and hope to rise naturally. Any experience that helps you feel connected reveals something about your authentic self. Any feeling of interconnection tells you that you're moving into the domain of the soul.

Make a commitment to pay attention to *when* you experience interconnection, for it's a sign of being on the right track. Also make a commitment to *create* these experiences by returning to the practices or activities that evoke that feeling. A spiritual practice, for example, prayer, as well as going to your church, synagogue, or mosque; doing yoga; meditating; singing; dancing; or volunteering could easily strengthen your essence and make it easier for you to hear that "still, small voice inside."

Your Radiant Life: Too Good to Be True

It's hard to imagine, but an extraordinary life change can be quite uncomplicated. If you just make a commitment to embrace the four *intentions* of clarity, integrity, courage, and compassion while paying attention to the four felt *experiences* of intuition, vitality, love, and connection, you can begin to reverse even the most extreme case of Inspiration Deficit Disorder *immediately.* You don't need to know what is next, and you don't even need to fully understand how you got to the place where you are—you don't need anything in order to begin right now.

If you don't believe it, try it and see. Answers and very specific changes will become clear as you follow the natural compass of your Essential Self.

Of course, simple is not always easy, and that's why this will take some time. When you follow the guidance of your Essential Self, a new, natural momentum will begin to work in your favor. At first *it will get uncomfortable* as you try new things, but soon your vital force will assist you in breaking old habits and becoming more present and intentional with each moment.

When you fully embrace your essence, your decisions, actions, intentions, talents, and sense of meaning will all be in alignment. It's the experience of total balance within—the very life force of your essence and Original Source will shine through your eyes. It sounds like a cliché, but it really is a spring in the step and a sparkle in the smile. It looks a lot like being in love; but it is wiser, more patient, confident, and unattached. *It is magnificent.* Just building the frequency of such moments in your weeks, days, and hours will bring you ever deeper into the richness of life.

> *"Now here is my secret. It is very simple. It is only with one's heart that one can see clearly. What is essential is invisible to the eye."*
>
> — ANTOINE DE SAINT-EXUPÉRY

◦◦◉◦◦

CHAPTER TWELVE

A Prescription for
Inspired Living: Ten Steps

*"My own prescription for health is less paperwork
and more running barefoot through the grass."*

— LESLIE GRIMUTTER

Doing What Works

In my work and training to help people live more inspired lives, I've noticed some general patterns and themes as to what feeds the Essential Self and what keeps many of us stuck. This chapter is a simple overview of the most important steps to ending Inspiration Deficit Disorder. (And in the next chapter, I'll point out the ten most common traps that get in our way and how to avoid them.)

As you read, consider taking notes and creating your own checklist, or use the one at the end of this chapter. I also provide online and downloadable tools on my Website that will help you walk through these steps. (If you'd like a workbook or other supporting information, please visit: **www.jonathanellerby.com**.) Keep the following tips in mind as you navigate each day and you'll guarantee positive results in your life.

Ten Steps to Nourish Your Essence

"Guard well your spare moments. They are like uncut diamonds. Discard them and their value will never be known. Improve them and they will become the brightest gems in a useful life."

— RALPH WALDO EMERSON

1. Have a Vision

Whatever change you seek, always *start with a vision* of what you want the experience and end result to look like. Don't be afraid to dream. Visualize your ideal life, and make sure it's aligned with the foundational qualities of an inspired individual (clarity, integrity, courage, and compassion) and that it also resonates according to the voice of your Essential Self (intuition, vitality, love, and connection).

Being *vision driven* doesn't mean that inspired living is *goal driven*. Goals are helpful, but they can become rigid sources of attachment and worry. Having a clear vision means that your life is intention based. The more explicit you are about your inner and outer intentions, the easier it will be to make beneficial choices and know when you're living in your essence (and when you aren't).

Inner intentions are statements like: *I will be more loving* [or *patient, comical,* or *forgiving*]. Circumstances have no impact on whether or not you can fulfill an inner intention—in fact, the harder the situation, the better the opportunity to practice what you aspire to.

Outer intentions are things that are more circumstantial and external. Here are some examples: *I will help reduce the number of homeless people in my city, I will spend more time with my parents,* or *I will drink less.* If you don't know what you want yet and your Essential Self isn't clear, then start with the feelings you desire more of in your life. Less stress? More joy? That's enough to get you started. Don't get too caught up in questions about purpose and think that the answer lies in a job or a relationship. Your purpose is to be the best expression of yourself, regardless of what you do.

A helpful exercise is to write a short paragraph that describes your ideal life one year from now. Use the present tense, and make it as inspiring as possible. Describe how you *will* feel about yourself and your relationships, as well as the ways in which you spend your time. Don't include any limits or doubts you may have in your personal progress. Remember to stay connected to your Essential Self as you write. Wishing for wealth and power, for example, may be aligned more with what your Persona desires.

For a truly inspiring and extraordinary vision, start by asking yourself: *What does life want from me? What is my greatest gift to the world? What does God want from me?* If you're willing to ask these kinds of questions, take a weekend and some quiet time to reflect. Feel your way into the answers, and try not to overthink it. Ask for guidance, and spend a lot of time listening within.

2. Make Inspired Decisions

Firmly commit to making as many decisions as possible from your essence. Following the four voices of the

Essential Self (discussed in the previous chapter), be sure that your sense of *intuition, vitality, love,* and *connection* are always in agreement with each and every choice you make. Integrity shows itself in everything you do, from how you treat strangers to how you communicate with loved ones and even in the things you buy. Be sure that whatever you choose, your soul is engaged.

Inspiration Deficit Disorder is created one decision at a time *and so is an inspired life.* Try to choose inspiration in every moment! Pay attention to how you make decisions. When faced with any choice, stop first, take a breath, and then step back and revisit your intentions. Check in with your essence before you take action.

3. Adopt Inspired Communication

Communication moves the world. The way you use your words (and your tone), body language, presence, and even your absence are all part of how you express yourself. You are not only communicating your ideas, but also your feelings and intentions. Every time you speak (or send an e-mail), you're also telling people how to treat you. If you communicate from your wounds, you'll generally cause others to respond from their woundedness; and if you're communicating from your superficial Persona, you'll get the same in return. When you speak from the heart, however, you'll most often receive a heartfelt reply.

A big part of inspired living is taking responsibility for your truth *and* your needs. Remember to embrace the key qualities of the essence: *clarity, integrity, courage,* and *compassion.* By doing so, regardless of the setting, you will always speak from your heart. You'll be able to manage your energy effectively and find the results of your communication satisfying. When you know you've offered your best, there can be no regrets.

Before important or emotionally charged conversations, take the time to walk through the steps of inspired communication. Try to formulate an intention and even a visualization of your performance. The goal in rehearsing a "charged" conversation isn't to control the outcome or achieve a certain response; it's about doing your best to be your best.

If you need to write down your thoughts first or have the conversation over the phone, give yourself permission to focus on what works best—as long as it's not only motivated by your wounds and reactions. Remember that effective communication is about conveying a message with clarity, integrity, courage, and compassion.

If you're certain that you'll react too hastily or become sidetracked in a particular setting or situation, explain your difficulty to the person you need to speak to. Ask for his or her understanding, and then in a mutually agreeable setting, speak your truth—no judgment, no blaming, and no speaking on behalf of others. Keep it simple; and if the response isn't what you want, take a few deep breaths and notice the emotions that rise to the surface. Feel the feelings until you gain a better perspective, then revisit your inspired decision-making strategy or communication steps. If it helps, step away from the situation and resist the temptation to justify your Wall or feed your Persona.

4. Allow Time for Fun

You need to have fun—often! And you need to get out of your busy mind—*often.* Not only does it help to develop a playful attitude during daily activities, but you also need to schedule time to relax and be creative *regularly.* The expression "Get out of your head!" sounds strange but requires little explanation. Think about what *fun* means to you, such as playing cards or sports, watching movies, going to the park, or hanging out at an art gallery. It doesn't matter what it is or if others find it entertaining—you need to enjoy it. Find something you can lose yourself in.

It's important not to always pick activities that have ulterior motives, such as career advancement or personal growth. Remember that plain old fun is critical to your well-being! Another dangerous common motive is escape, but what you do for soulful pleasure should be engaging, not numbing. When you take time for yourself, you should feel even more fulfilled and in touch with your essence—not hollow and disconnected.

An ideal form of recreation for people with Inspiration Deficit Disorder is to be more creative and get involved in something artistic. Playing a sport can also be helpful, but often can become too competitive and feed your Persona. If you want to choose a sport to feed your essence, that's fine, but try playing so that there isn't a winner or one single "right way" to score. The bottom line is to promote inner peace and lots of laughter. You might also try shifting your attitude about a sport you already know and love. Work to experience it for the joy and pleasure, not from a place of striving to be perfect. Other ideas include taking a class in cooking or watercolor painting; gardening; taking walks in nature; going fishing; learning to play chess or bridge; playing on a team; joining a book club; or taking up a new craft, such as knitting, woodworking, or scrapbooking.

The key word is *fun,* not indulgent. You need to be affirmed in delight, meaning that enjoying simple pleasures will remind you of the *joy* of living. One of the most important things you need to understand about your essence is that when you strengthen *any* part of it, you strengthen *all* of it! The Persona-driven life is easily compartmentalized—keeping work from home life, from personal goals, and so on. Each aspect of a Persona-driven life can excel at the expense of the others.

When it comes to knowing your purpose or finding your "self" again, you don't need all the answers—just start by strengthening your connection to your essence and in time it will grow strong and clear enough to hear with ease. It's hard for many to imagine, but having fun, feeding your passions, and engaging your talents are simple steps that will take you to the bigger answers you seek.

5. Keep Learning; Be Curious

The hallmark of a growing, lively soul is openness to new ideas and experiences. The moment you ignore or disregard other views and perspectives, know that you're slipping into your Persona. Hatred, judgment, narrowness, egotism, and close-minded thinking are *not* functions of the Essential Self. They aren't natural to who you are, although with a little wounding and a lot of external influences, a shift away from the Essential Self can feel deep rooted. Resistance to new thoughts and ways of thinking are typically an expression of insecurity and fear.

When you feel challenged by a different point of view, take a deep breath and try to be curious instead of jumping to conclusions. Ask questions, and seek to understand the position from a broader perspective.

If you feel like nothing is new or surprising in your life, you may want to take a class or train in some other new subject, craft, or skill. It doesn't have to cost much— attend a lecture at your local library or community center, for example. There are always ways to expand your worldview. Even if you're the best at what you do, learn it from a fresh perspective, such as viewing things with a beginner's mind or studying something outside your area of knowledge. Exposure to diversity is transformative. Learning should be a lifelong journey; life is an endless discovery process.

6. Help Out

There's no question that one of the most universal qualities taught by spiritual teachers of all nations and all times is to *be of service in the world.* A life lived only for your own benefit is an existence that's cut off from the fullness of the world. If each person were to ask, *How can I uniquely and powerfully make a difference in the world?* and acted on the answer, without doubt, the world would be a dramatically different place.

Volunteering by giving your time and energy (more than sending money) is a beautiful and meaningful way to become inspired. Giving without a desire for gain or compensation enables you to feel the genuine rewards of gratitude, connection, humility, and respect.

Find a cause you believe in, such as promoting literacy or animal-rights issues; assisting refugees; fighting poverty, drug abuse, or water pollution; helping war veterans; creating green spaces in urban centers; or anything else. Whatever the cause, learn more about it, get motivated, and get involved. When you give your own energy from your Essential Self, you will connect with the Essential Self of those you serve. When that happens, something amazing emerges: the awakening of a sense of The Sacred and the precious nature of life, which is truly revitalizing.

7. Spend More Time in Nature

Even if it's not typically your "cup of tea," spend more time in nature. Do so according to your own interests and comfort level. Try a garden, city park, national park, campground, wilderness program, the beach, the desert, the mountains, a greenhouse, a farm . . . whatever suits you best. The point is to spend more time outside—weekly or, at the very least, monthly. It may be hard to believe this, unless you've experienced it firsthand, but the natural world is already tuned in to the rhythm and melody of *your* essence. Nature is, without a doubt, the best place for most people to connect with their Essential Self.

There are so many ways to be in nature: sitting, walking, running, picnicking, hiking, bird-watching, or even growing your own garden at home. (As an example, a fantastic Website that provides great ideas and ways to make something as simple as gardening into a magical experience is **http://awaytogarden.com**).

In late 2009, I created a survey about modern spirituality (you can still participate at **www.thespirituality survey.com**). One of the questions is: "What is the most naturally spiritual place? Where do you most often and naturally feel a strong sense of spiritual connection, or feelings of The Sacred?" As of this writing, over 1,500 people have replied, and over 75 percent of them said that nature (over "a religious place of worship" or any-where else) was where they most often felt a sense of something spiritual and restoring. This came as no sur-prise since the world's spiritual and healing traditions are all filled with stories, teachings, and metaphors that present the natural world as the ultimate teacher and setting for transformation. The prophetic visions, divine revelations, and great awakenings of the world's spiri-tual masters—such as Jesus, Moses, Buddha, Moham-med, and nearly all others—took place in the heart of the wilderness.

The natural world follows the rhythms of the Origi-nal Source, and *if you spend enough time in nature, you will automatically fall into harmony with your essence.* There's a kind of gravity that will pull you out of the "business" of life, out of your Persona, and into a sense of greater peace and of what matters most. In the Inspired-Living Resources section of this book, you'll find even more opportunities to use the natural world as a setting for growth and personal empowerment.

8. Build Community:
Fellowship, Safety, and Connection

One of the oldest principles of inspired living is also one of the most misunderstood. *Seek a like-minded community.* This could mean focusing on specific friends you already have; joining a support group; getting in-volved in a spiritual community; starting a book club; or becoming a member of an online group where people are able to meet and network. (At my own Website, **www .jonathanellerby.com**, we help members find these kinds of resources. I also recommend the networking opportunities at **www.tokenrock.com, www.healyour life.com,** and **www.beliefnet.com**; however, these sites have a strong personal growth and spirituality focus and may not be for everyone.)

Finding this kind of community is important because the momentum of old habits is hard to face alone. To effect the most change, we often need new energy, positive encouragement, and the opportunity to exchange fresh ideas with others who share a similar intention or worldview.

Looking back to Part I of this book, you may recall the story of your birth and your origin, a mysterious source and force of creative potential. Since the direct experience of this Original Source feels like *love and connection,* then any experience of a relationship of genuine safety, love, and connection will draw you back to your essence. This is the heart of true family, true therapy, true love, and true healing. In the most powerful healing and treatment programs I've ever studied or experienced, I've found one common theme: a community of love and connection. I've witnessed it work to help heal addiction, trauma, violent behavior, and self-hatred. It takes time, as well as a circle of willing hearts.

Be cautious, however, not to judge those who are not a natural support to you or reject those who are unlike you. Ensuring that you have the support you need doesn't mean you have to lose or attack everyone who doesn't qualify as like-minded. Remember that joining a group or organization you're passionate about doesn't mean that everyone else is wrong. Be careful not to let your Persona overtake your sense of pride, or soon you'll turn your support circle into a gang who thinks that their way is the only way.

9. Develop a Spiritual Practice:
Slow Down and Get Connected

The idea of a spiritual practice generates a strong re-action of resistance in many people. Even the term *spirituality* repels some and at least confuses others. It sounds like something *other* people do, and even then, it isn't clear exactly what they do. In my book *Return to The Sacred* as well as my audio program, *Your Spiritual Personality,* I go into great depth explaining the why's and how's of spiritual practice. I also discuss many of the most universally effective and appealing practices. For simplicity, however, *let's call any activity that helps you to slow down and feel a sense of peace and connection a spiritual practice.*

Ideally, this would be an activity you do regularly, intentionally, and outside of normal responsibilities. Being with my son is a spiritual experience for me, but it doesn't really count as a distinct time-out away from my roles and expectations. Daily meditations, breathing exercises, prayer, church services, yoga, contemplative walks, gardening, tai chi, mindfulness exercises, and even golf or dance could all qualify as spiritual practices to explore.

Since the function of your practice is to remind you of your essence and offer you a taste of inner wisdom and serenity, it's important to return to it as often as possible. A spiritual practice you engage in once a week or month—if it's the only practice you have—will rarely be enough to sustain a truly inspired life. Find something simple you can do every day, and then try a more involved activity once or twice a week.

Ask yourself what types of things help you feel most at peace. What connects you to God (or your own sense of what is sacred and essential)? If you don't know where to begin, start exploring what's available in your area. In the meantime, make an effort to set aside five minutes every day for a simple practice. You might like to try the following:

1. Find a quiet place where you won't be interrupted (even if it needs to be a bathroom in your busy house or outside on an apartment balcony—find a space).

2. Spend two minutes doing nothing but breathing. In and out through your nose only, if possible. You should be seated comfortably with your back straight. Try to draw your breath down into the region of your belly, not into your upper chest. This may take some practice. (I have a video called *Breathing 101* on my Website that explains this breathing style.)

3. After your two minutes of breathing, notice yourself relaxing and turn your attention to what you feel grateful for. After about a minute or so of reflecting on all the big and little things that you're thankful for, pause for another moment and pay attention to how you feel.

4. Finally, shift your attention to your Essential Self and the vision you've created for yourself. Who do you intend to be today? How will you show the highest and best of yourself? What are your inner and outer intentions? Recommit . . . *and then take a deep breath and begin your day.*

If you're really struggling with this *critical* step of developing a regular spiritual practice, you might try using some "support." Creative visualization products by

NewReality (**www.newreality.com**) provide great ways to slow down the mind and body. Companies like this one offer both the technology and the programming to help you achieve the state of mind you seek using state-of-the-art science. Much of the music by Jonathan Goldman (**www.healingsounds.com**) has been designed to aid meditation and deep relaxation. You might also check out the amazing collection of relaxation and meditation music by Dean and Dudley Evenson (**www .soundings.com**).

A good set of headphones and ten minutes of meditative music while sitting in a quiet, comfortable place (or even during a walk) can be an effective way of exploring a spiritual practice. In addition, I have a host of free meditations, visualizations, and breathing exercises on my Website. If you'd like some diversity of instruction, try out this very useful site: **www.the meditationmind.com**.

10. Respect Your Body

It's easy to think that inspired living is only about inner intentions, pure ideas, and philosophies of kindness. It's natural for some to think that the inner work is enough, but it's not. An inspired life is a *whole* life, meaning that you also honor and respect your body.

Your body and the ways in which you interact with the world are unforgettable facets of the human experience. The way you eat, rest, and exercise; how you manage your time and space; and your use of pharmaceutical medicine and nutritional supplements are all examples of physical factors that impact your energy and mood.

Your general health and fitness is strongly linked to your emotional and spiritual well-being.

The health of your body directly impacts your disposition, energy levels, motivation, and self-concept. Take the time to find what parts of your body may need healing and rehabilitation. Then begin a lifestyle of healing and prevention. Prevention is about focusing on being vibrant and healthy for as long as possible rather than waiting to "fix" something.

At Canyon Ranch, where I work as the Spiritual Program Director, we've been helping people understand these best practices of prevention for more than 30 years. You can also find great information and guidance through the magazines *Natural Health* and *Body+Soul*. I highly recommend the following Websites to help you learn more about what's available to you: **www.drweil.com**, **www.wholeliving.com**, and **www.naturalhealthmag.com**. Moreover, on my site, you'll find links to these sites as well as access to the health and fitness professionals I know and trust who can help you create wellness plans and get your physical journey of vitality under way.

There was a time in my life when I felt I could do all my own health research and set my own wellness plans. Over time I came to learn that no one person can know all the details of a specialist in every field of knowledge important to his or her own life. Even after years of personal experimenting, I still go to experts whenever I can for coaching, training, or guidance.

As an example, since my early 20s I have been very attentive to my physical fitness. After a hiatus from the gym to focus on our newborn and the release of a book, I was fortunate to meet Brandon Wagner, a leading fitness professional (**www.fitspecialists.com**). With years of experience and training in leading exercise techniques and exercise physiology research, Brandon accelerated my return to wellness in a way that was safe, fun, and efficient. Together, we accomplished much more than I could have alone.

Don't be afraid to ask for help or drop in at a local gym, community center, or hospital for a free public educational session or to find a professional to help you. (Chapter 14 will explore this idea in greater depth.)

In addition, try using the "Top-Ten Tips Checklist" to help you create your own inspired-living prescription.

Top-Ten Tips Checklist

Keep this handy. Consider making a copy of this checklist so that you can fill it out and refer to it often. Some people like to tack this up on a wall in their bedroom, bathroom, or office. By doing so, you can easily evaluate how you're doing on a weekly basis.

Monitor your progress. Rate your performance of each tip on a scale from 1 to 5:

> 5 = You're exceeding your expectations
>
> 4 = You're fulfilling your commitments
>
> 3 = You're making an effort regularly, but it's not consistent
>
> 2 = You may have good intentions, but they're rarely acted upon
>
> 1 = You've abandoned your commitment entirely

Review and refine. I suggest that you mark the first day of each month on your calendar for the next six months as a reminder to sit down and review and refine your answers. It's okay to create new answers. Keep in mind that the ranking process is to help you see your progress and give yourself valuable feedback; it's not a tool for self-judgment or blame.

____ *Have a vision:* I have a written vision that inspires me and keeps me motivated and on track.

____ *Make inspired decisions:* I'm making a daily effort to be aware of how I make decisions and to pay more attention to my energy, sense of connection, and feelings of compassion. I trust my intuition.

___ *Adopt inspired communication:* I communicate with clarity, integrity, courage, and compassion.

___ *Allow time for fun:* I take time each week to _____ just for the fun of it.

___ *Keep learning; be curious:* Right now, I'm interested in _____, and I'm taking the following steps to learn more: _____.

___ *Help out:* I give back to my world and community by _____.

___ *Spend more time in nature:* I've identified my favorite way to be in nature, which is _____. I make time to do this _____ times a month.

___ *Build community:* I feel loved, supported, and encouraged by _____. I connect with them regularly.

___ *Develop a spiritual practice:* Every day I slow down by _____. Each week I find a deeper peace and connection by _____.

___ *Respect your body:* I've had a recent checkup, and I'm confident in my wellness plan, which includes: _____.

◎◎◉◎◎

CHAPTER THIRTEEN

Ten Traps That Get in the Way of Inspired Living

"All growth is a leap in the dark, a spontaneous, unpremeditated act without benefit of experience."

— HENRY MILLER

Watch Your Step!

For every trick, there is always a trap. Sadly, an inspired life is about as easy to have as it is *not* to have. There are many natural distractions and misconceptions that keep people stuck. In this chapter, I've compiled the top-ten ways that our Walls, Personas, and energy hooks tend to catch us off guard and keep us from fully embracing our essence.

This is a list you'll want to review once a week or whenever you're feeling out of alignment with your Essential Self. Take a close look at yourself; and as you read, honestly evaluate which traps you may have fallen into. Although these are common, know that you *can* take charge and pull yourself out.

1. Procrastination

It seems harmless when you're in the middle of doing it, but procrastination can be a showstopper when it comes to transformation. The bottom line is that you end up putting off a choice or action to a later date when there's *really* no good reason not to do it today. As you've been reading this book, you may have thought, *Oh yes, I should do more of that,* or *I would like to do more of this.* The trouble lies in the rationalizations of the Persona and the Wall of Wounding—they'll do anything to protect themselves and keep the Essential Self hidden.

The simple rule of inspired living is this: Whenever you can choose differently, do so. No debate. No delay. Sometimes a client will be facing a major decision in his or her life and will ask me: "When should I tell him about this?" or "When should I start?" and I'll almost always answer: "How about today?" When it comes to turning your life upside down, there's never a perfect moment. Any time is a good time . . . *just start!*

2. Guilt and the Need for Permission

If I added up all the energy that the people I see and know spend on guilt and a lack of personal permission, I'd have enough electricity to solve the world's energy crisis forever! Another common and extraordinarily powerful obstacle to our success and progress in life is the guilt we feel for doing things for ourselves instead of always making choices that put others first. For the most part, society has worked hard to ensure that living from the essence has become misunderstood as a *selfish* thing. We even rehearse the expectations of others: "I can't leave work on time—everyone else stays late!" or

"What kind of a mother has someone else pick her kids up while she goes to an art class or does yoga?"

It doesn't really matter why you feel guilty. If you *know* in your heart of hearts what you need to do, then you must find a way to do it. Here are some tips to help you overcome your guilt and need for permission:

- Make a list naming all the benefits of what you want to do.

- Write down all the costs (negative effects) of you *not* doing what you want to do.

- Use positive affirmations (self-talk), such as: *I deserve this. Doing this is good for my health. If I am at my best, then I can share my best with others.*

- Take the time to honor and explore your feelings through discussion with a coach, friend, or therapist. Then use their support to begin your commitment.

Keep one of these two little sayings in mind:

- *Guilt will make me wilt, but permission is my decision!*

- *What others think of me is none of my business.*

3. The Fear of Being Uncomfortable

People who are familiar with my work often want to know what secrets and magical things I've picked up over the years of traveling and living among cultures around the world. While I've experienced extraordinary events, studied potent philosophies, and even dabbled in the miraculous, the most cherished gift I received from all my teachers is the *ability to accept and be okay with being uncomfortable.*

The odd thing about being uncomfortable is that most people downplay the discomfort they're *familiar* with (such as a poor relationship, stressful job, or sense of confusion). They choose the struggle they know over the effort of change. When we try to make changes that threaten our Wall of Wounding, we generally end up returning to the discomfort we know instead of facing the unresolved emotion of the past. It's a poor trade that can keep us stuck forever. If we're going to be uncomfortable, we might as well pick the discomfort that will set us free!

Whenever you end a habit, addiction, or cycle of nonessential behavior, you *will* feel uncomfortable. You'll be at a loss for energy. You'll be challenging your stories of life and probably feel the emotion of whatever wound has been keeping the old behavior in place. That is called *progress!*

Allow the discomfort you experience during change to be a sign that you're on track (assuming it's essence driven) and on the path to wholeness. The biggest error you can make is to stop and second-guess yourself every time you run into an awkward feeling.

4. Avoiding, Denying, or Repressing Emotions

More than the general discomfort of change, most people fear the actual experience of emotions, particularly when it comes to their Wall of Wounding. If you've left old feelings unaddressed or hidden away deep within, you've probably already decided that they'll be too overwhelming to face. The fear of being consumed or overcome by sadness, loss, anger, regret, or pain is natural, although not worth acting on. When you repress an emotion (don't feel it), you actually lock it into your body and store it for later. When you react and later express it *at* people, then you just feed it. The solution lies in between: *you must feel it.*

Just because you're afraid to admit a feeling or are worried that it will swallow you whole doesn't mean you have an excuse to continue avoiding it. It will only linger and wait until you can or have to face it. The longer you put it off, the more unpredictable and uncontrollable the emotion will be when you finally meet it face-to-face.

When you break or undo the energy hooks from your life, that energy will spill out, leaving you with a loss of power. Emotions such as sadness, anger, loneliness, shame, guilt, and regret all lie just below the surface of the Persona. Your energy hooks and habits keep you distracted (such as drinking too much, working too hard, helping everyone else but yourself, and so on) so you don't have to feel them. As a result, a false sense of comfort sets in. Genuine healing and change come by experiencing and moving through your emotions. Remember that *emotions are energy;* and if they aren't released or resolved, they'll remain stuck in your body, holding old, limiting beliefs in place.

As my longtime mentor and second father Wanagi Wachi has always said, "Healing comes through feeling." In order to overcome and release emotions, the simple task is to feel them. This doesn't mean to act on them—just experience them. Be sad. Be angry. Be jealous. Listening to music, writing in your journal, exercising, or talking to a friend can help you work through the emotion. Stay with it as long as you can, keeping in mind that it's *just* a feeling. It will pass. Eventually, you'll realize that most of your stories concerning it were wrong. If you allow your emotions the time and energy they need to resolve, more often than not they'll transform on their own, leaving you with new insights.

5. Misunderstanding Physical Symptoms During Change

Emotions and the energy of your essence are fluid and always moving. When there is wounding—or what some people call an "emotional block"—there is always a congestion of energy. If unexpressed, over time the old pain and disconnect will resurface somewhere in your body. Remember that your body's energy isn't a symbolic idea but a real, subtle force. Many of the earlier stories in the book illustrated the ways in which lifestyle changes and emotional releases helped people not only feel happier, but also become physically healthier.

Don't be surprised if you experience temporary physical symptoms while you go through a major transition from Persona-based energy hooks to soul power. I like to use the metaphor of a house that draws its electric power from a city grid. If one day the home owners choose to switch to a renewable, personally managed source of power, they may have to endure a dark night or two and reset a few appliances during the changeover. The shift in power may require a temporary surge or outage.

A change in appetite or energy level; the need for more sleep or bodywork (such as massage); or a hypersensitivity to certain types of people, places, and things may all naturally follow a radical time of inner change. Be patient, drink lots of water, and get plenty of rest. Eat a nutrient-rich diet, avoid junk foods and recreational drugs (including too much alcohol), consider supplements, and don't be afraid to allow yourself to be nurtured and pampered a bit. If you need extra time for yourself during your transition, take it. Simple things like salt baths and aromatherapy can be a great help as well (I recommend products from **www.lotuswei.com**).

This stage won't last forever. The longer you resist it or the more you panic about it, the longer it will last. If physical symptoms persist, see your family doctor. Be sure to explain all the change that's going on in your life as a part of your discussion about the physical symptoms that concern you.

6. Overthinking

Inspired living doesn't always make sense. No one can really explain why a relationship might look great on paper but not in real life. There are certain jobs that all logic would say you should love, but you won't. It's the same as to how you can't quite explain why you love the music that makes your heart soar or the flavor of ice cream that causes you to close your eyes in delight with every taste. The heart knows what it wants, and it often makes no sense. Intuition, creativity, and listening are all imperative in creating an inspired life.

The power of the mind to organize, strategize, and break things down into steps is vital to an essential-living plan, but it is of little help to your advancement. The more concrete and measurable your action plan is, the more likely you are to succeed. Your mind has an important job! Its role, however, is to serve the soul— not the other way around. Your essence is the vision holder, the part of you that knows your direction and purpose. The mind can make it come true because it's a doer. Although if you ask the doer to create the vision or lead the ship, you'll end up in trouble fast because it will always fall prey to the Persona.

The key is to place your intuitive, heartfelt vision first, and then let the mind serve it. The more time you spend "out of your mind" in relaxation, recreation, spiritual practice, and an embrace of the moment *as it is,* the better off you will be. The less you think about how and what you should be, the clearer it will become. Learn to quiet your thoughts. Your Essential Self speaks through experience and the four voices of the essence outlined earlier: intuition, vitality, love, and connection.

7. Trying to Be Perfect

Inspired living isn't about being perfect, always right, or righteous—it's about being human, humble, and willing to explore life as it unfolds. Too often people turn their search for peace and personal growth into a new Persona story and energy hook. Without yoga, church, or their self-help books, they feel lost. All their conversations have to be about healing, and their strong focus and commitment turns into a new addiction. On the inspired road, however, good enough is good enough.

Think of your life as a piece of art and experiment with colors, textures, and shades. Notice how you can turn an error into a valuable lesson or a masterpiece. Now think of your existence from a scientific perspective and create a hypothesis. Then test it out! If it works, ask yourself how it feels, and be open to the results. Don't fake the data—let life show you what works best.

Perfection is an illusion of the Persona. It's an obsession with an idealized future state that never arrives. It attempts to make static things change and manipulate situations that aren't under your control. The only perfection you need to know is the Original Source and essence that is you. These are perfect and yet so mysterious that you'll spend your life trying to understand them. There is no end to the self or Spirit that forms all of humanity.

Release the self-judgment that is rooted behind the desire to be perfect. Remember that all progress is to be celebrated. Make your decisions from a place of intention and not from a place of judgment or your Persona, Wall, and energy hooks. Address what you can, and accept your limits. You don't have to fix everything all at once.

8. Confusing Attachment, Pleasing, and Approval for Love

Amazingly, love (or the idea of it) can end up being a huge problem in the process of awakening to your greatest life. Don't confuse the affection you feel for someone with your desire to have his or her constant approval. And don't reverse a decision just because you fear that someone you care about will no longer accept the new you.

True love is dynamic: it grows, waxes, and wanes, continually evolving and adapting. If you're not living your essence fully, the people who love you and understand compassion will want you to be fulfilled. If not, they either don't understand yet or simply can't. Regardless, you're choosing between health and despair. Your suffering serves no one.

People and relationships can be energy hooks. You can actually feel entwined and in love (or infatuated) with individuals who aren't good for you. In fact, they're the ones who are the easiest to become involved with! That often isn't love; it's codependency. Yes, it's possible to have both love and codependency, and it's also possible to shift your relationship to a place where you're both relating from your essence. You can apply all the principles in this book to a couple (or a family or a business) as easily as to an individual. Pay special attention to the sections on inspired communication and decision making.

Interestingly enough, the misunderstandings of love can be at the root of a Persona-motivated change that's mistaken as an essence-based decision. Long relationships in marriage, work, and even family will go through cycles. The ups and downs of all the individuals involved won't always match one another. When they don't, you may be tempted to use a lack of inspired living as an excuse to jump ship. Be careful, for your ship may just be in a storm and not really sinking. You'll know you've made a serious mistake when the clouds part and you're lost at sea, mourning what you abandoned.

Be watchful of the extent to which your relationships influence you. Since an inspired life is soul centered, you don't have to refer to others' needs to determine what to do next. At the same time, out of a sense of respect and interconnection, you won't act ignorantly or in a cruel spirit, either. There's nothing soulful about that. When it comes to relationship complications, it's a good idea to seek guidance and advice from a professional. The heart is a complex domain. It's often too difficult to sort out emotions with the person you may be struggling with.

9. Impatience

I can virtually promise that if you embrace the ten keys for inspired living, the four soul senses (the voices of your Essential Self), and the four qualities that create the foundation of an inspired individual (or even half of these things), you'll experience immediate transformation. But don't let the promise of a quick change feed the tendency to be impatient. Despite society's need for instant gratification, the deeper levels of inspired living take time to unfold and become established.

If you're in the process of making life changes, ask yourself how long it took to reach your current state. Remember that your Wall was built over many years, and your habits didn't take hold overnight. There is an old Zen expression that says, "Fall down seven times, get up eight." Be patient, persevere, and allow time for your great awakening. Keep in mind that unexpected things will show up along the way.

The guidelines and priorities that I recommend in the next chapters are about focus, not expectation or control. Choose to use your time as an ally rather than an enemy of yourself. Trust that if you're moving into an essence-centered life, then surrender, openness, and acceptance of a higher wisdom and process are all a part of the experience. Inspired living is not a desire, but a calling—something that you co-create with the universe instead of attempting to will it into being. Genuine inspiration is always happening: you just need to relax, have faith in the promptings of your essence, and get out of the way.

10. Labeling All Stress as Bad

After all this talk of Inspiration Deficit Disorder and balanced living, it's important to know that *it is okay to choose stress at times.* Lots of wonderful things involve stress, and even though you don't want those stressful periods and reactions to last or become a lifestyle, there is no harm in consciously embracing stress for short periods of time.

For example, in writing this book, my wife and I discussed that I'd need to put in extra hours of work and that it would be demanding on me and our family. It was a stressful process at times, but we knew that and accepted it from the start. All the important things in life remained a priority, and I temporarily cut back or cut out some less-important things. My family life always came first, and sometimes it was tested by the additional demands on my time and energy. This was an intentional choice made with full awareness of the limited timeline and sacrifice. It was all a choice and a design, which made it an inspired process.

Moving homes, getting married, starting your dream job, or creating a new life plan can be stressful, even though they are also all wonderful things. Stress is a problem when it feels unstoppable, out of control, or is impacting your health and habits. Don't make excuses for your stress in order to allow it, yet you also shouldn't expect yourself to always be stress free. You are still human, so don't forget that stress is a part of life. A little stress that you choose and monitor is always okay in an inspired life.

Embracing Change

> *"One does not discover new lands without consenting to lose sight of the shore for a very long time."*
>
> — ANDRÉ GIDE

Embracing change isn't always easy, which is why so many people stay stuck. The other major factor is that we often live with illusions of what change *should* be like. Knowing the traps not only helps us avoid them, but it also feeds our sense of self-acceptance through the awareness that it's totally natural to make mistakes and get trapped from time to time along the way.

More than awareness alone, having a partner, sponsor, friend, or coach who can help you see when you get stuck and offer support is vital. The next chapter stresses the importance of involving the assistance and expertise of others. Just because the Essential Self carries all the wisdom and direction you need, it doesn't mean that you'll always see it on your own. Your essence thrives on interconnection in one form or another.

◎◎◉◎◎

CHAPTER FOURTEEN

A Little Help Can Help a Lot: Healing from the Outside In

"A lot of people say they want to get out of pain, and I'm sure that's true, but they aren't willing to make healing a high priority. They aren't willing to look inside to see the source of their pain in order to deal with it."

— LINDSAY WAGNER

The Whole Self

The most effective way to end stress, low energy, bad habits, and just about any other challenge you can think of begins within. Your Essential Self carries the formula for your healing, joy, and greatest capacity to create. An effort that attempts to negate the Essential Self is doomed from the start. True life balance and inspired living, however, can't all be internal or driven by the self and spirit alone. You were born into a specific body, community, and culture. In any process of transformation, you will likely need some support, guidance, coaching, counseling, and resources from others. You may not need all of these things in large amounts, but if you're human, you'll need at least some amount of them.

Human health is *holistic,* meaning that it isn't reducible to a collection of parts, but that the sum of the parts results in a greater whole in which all the parts are interconnected and engaged. Much like a car engine, without some parts you can still drive it—perhaps poorly or not for very long. Without other parts, though, you can't even get the motor running. The human system has millions of "parts," yet there are four distinct ones that must be involved in any change:

1. *Mental* (the world of your thoughts, ideas, attitudes, stories, and thinking)

2. *Physical* (the world of your body, diet, exercise, rest, mobility, and physical health)

3. *Emotional* (the world of your feelings, such as happiness, sadness, anger, fear, joy, and so on)

4. *Spiritual* (the world of your essence and connection to a Higher Power and the subtle energies and unseen forces of life)

Having worked in Western health-care settings and health resorts for years, I've seen, again and again, how the neglect of any one of these areas can come at a cost to the whole person. For example, I've watched people on diets who struggle because they lack the bigger picture to manifest their achievements. As long as they still think poorly of themselves, have an expectation to fail, or are surrounded by others who don't support their best interests, then any progress will soon retreat. I've also observed individuals endlessly try to mend a relationship when they've failed to recognize a physical health condition that's complicating their moods and energy levels. Many men and women who really want to change a job or life path are burdened by their poor diet and lack of exercise. Their motivation is weighed down by their general lack of self-care.

Even when healing from physical injury or in treating a chronic health condition, the intangible elements of mind, heart, and soul carry a far greater effect than most know or would admit. Many of the stories of people's transformations earlier in the book feature elements of physical imbalance that seem to have resulted from their lack of authenticity in life. In the same respect, some of the stories show how individuals with physical conditions can beat the odds by enlisting the power of their essence.

Holistic Self-Awareness

Regardless of the vision of life that your essence provides, be sure you approach your transformation thoroughly and completely. Try to get in the habit of doing a holistic self-review as often as possible—daily or throughout the day. This means that you take a few moments to stop, take a deep breath, and slow down until you can become aware of whatever you are experiencing in your body, mind, heart, and soul. Try out the "Holistic Check-in" on the following pages.

HOLISTIC CHECK-IN

At least once a day, and ideally whenever you feel challenged, practice doing a holistic self-review. This means that you set aside some time to become aware of what is going on in your body, mind, heart, and soul.

— While sitting quietly, take seven deep breaths. Each one should come in through the nose and move down toward the belly. Imagine that you're filling your belly with air as you inhale. Try not to breathe into your shoulders or chest.

— After you feel relaxed, like you've "slowed down," ask yourself the following questions and take a moment to notice what you become aware of. Give yourself time until you have an answer for each one. Use the questions in the order they've been presented here. You may like to journal your reply.

1. **Body:** *What physical sensations am I experiencing right now?*

Take a deeper look:

- *Can I feel my heart rate?*
- *What temperature am I experiencing?*
- *Where am I tight? Can I relax it?*
- *Am I making the best possible choices for my physical health and vitality?*

2. **Mind:** *What story am I telling myself about this situation?*

Take a deeper look:

- *Is what I'm thinking absolutely true or just my idea of truth?*

- *Am I dwelling in the past or future?*
- *What is the pace of my thinking? Is it hurried, worried, or clear?*
- *Am I judging?*

3. **Heart:** *What emotions did this situation raise in me?*

Take a deeper look:

- *Which emotions were the strongest?*
- *Do I need some time to just "feel" these emotions before I say/do anything?*
- *Are these emotions appropriate for this situation? Am I overreacting or underacting?*
- *Are these emotions related to or reminding me of something else or another time? If so, when did I first have an emotional experience like this one?*

4. **Soul:** *What is my highest intention for this situation?*

Take a deeper look:

- *What is the most loving and empowering next step?*
- *Is my reaction supporting my vitality and intention?*
- *What is the highest good of all involved in this case?*
- *How does my understanding of my essence and a Higher Power factor into this?*
- *What next step would have the most integrity?*

A Holistic Weekly Review

Until you are in a healthy habit, try this expanded question set once a week.

1. **Body:**

    • *Am I sleeping enough and not too much?*

    • *Am I eating healthy foods that work well with my body?*

    • *Am I moving enough and getting proper exercise?*

    • *Do I spend enough quality time in nature?*

    • *Do I have any injuries or concerns I should have checked out?*

2. **Mind:**

    • *When I reflect on my attitude lately, am I maintaining a balanced sense of:*

    Curiosity
    Self-awareness
    Optimism
    Neutrality
    Open-mindedness

    • *Do I have interests yet to explore or learn more about?*

3. **Heart:**

    • *Am I satisfied with my relationships? How am I being treated, and how am I treating others?*

    • *Am I generally content and happy with my choices?*

- *Is there an active emotional cycle that I'm struggling with right now?*

- *Where am I most emotionally nurtured and fed?*

4. **Soul:**

   - *Am I living my truth?*

   - *Am I connecting with my deepest sense and expression of self?*

   - *Am I making a difference in the world, even if it's small?*

   - *Do I feel a connection to something greater?*

   - *Am I committed to a spiritual practice, or am I taking time to do what feeds my essence the most?*

Healing and Relationships

Having researched the nature of healing and change in cultures around the world, it has become clear to me that the notion of healing as a solo act is a very recent idea. In ancient traditions, our ancestors knew that healing was always a community event on some levels.

As you make changes from within, you also change the ways in which you relate to others; and as you change how you relate to others, you change them and how they treat you. You cannot make changes without impacting the family, work, or social systems you're a part of. Whether you like it or not, or whether you feel alone or not, your change impacts others.

Expect Your Relationships to Be Impacted

Not everyone you know will love the change you seek. Some will celebrate it, and some will feel threatened by it. Expect people to be uncomfortable because that's a natural part of the process. You're changing something that is familiar to them: *you*. Don't be surprised if some people even react negatively to a positive change that they've been encouraging you to make. Remember that change creates discomfort. If you can, talk to the people who are impacted. Ask them how they're feeling and offer your support.

Tell People What You're Doing

Many of us feel shy about the aspirations we have or cautious about sharing them too soon. However, keeping your intentions to yourself reduces your sense of investment and accountability. Tell the people who are important to you what you're trying to accomplish in your life. You might have to explain that you're drinking less alcohol for your health, gossiping less for your peace of mind, or taking more time for art or spiritual practice for your serenity. It's okay to ask them to understand and lend their support. Loved ones really should at least try not to get in the way of your efforts to change, and at the most, they should attempt to help keep you on track.

Find an Inspiration Mate

Try to find a friend, sponsor, or buddy who is working toward the same or similar goals. More than a community of support, an individual who serves as your cheerleader, motivator, and sounding board is invaluable.

When you get off track in your mind or actions, have someone close at hand you can turn to.

In an earlier chapter, I mentioned some online networking opportunities, but nothing replaces a transformation support who can sit across the table from you or accompany you on a walk. You might check out some local workshops, lectures, or book signings where you could meet like-minded people.

Don't Assume That Everyone Will Get It

It really is okay if the people in your life don't understand what you're trying to accomplish. Oftentimes they won't. Precisely because they're a part of your old system and haven't helped you become free yet, they won't understand what your soul needs. The hardest moments may come when the people you know, love, and trust challenge you by claiming that *they* know you better than *you* do. I've heard these stories time and time again, so be wary. The following are examples of some of the things that loving friends and family members say to those who are on a quest to embrace an inspired life:

- "*You* aren't the kind of person to take a dance class [or other new activity]. I just can't see it."

- "You were never good at painting, so why try now?"

- "I just don't want you to get hurt trying something new."

- "It sounds like a lot of New Age, woo-woo, self-help junk."

- "I thought you were a professional!"

- "I thought you were a good Christian."

- "What will _____ [Mom, Dad, and so on] say?"
- "Your kids won't know who you are."
- "It might change our relationship."
- "What if it doesn't work out?"
- "Why change what you have? Isn't it enough for you?"
- "Don't you think you're being selfish?"

Much worse than what others may say, you also have to keep in mind what your Persona, energy hooks, and Wall of Wounding are telling you. Perhaps *you* are the one who's thinking these things!

Some Relationships Will End or Change Forever

As you become more soulful, you will find that the soulful connections in your life will deepen quickly and easily. Some people who used to be on the edge of your life will move into the center, and some who were at the center will have to move out to the edge or beyond. If you have advanced Inspiration Deficit Disorder, it really doesn't matter what your close relationships require from you. If it isn't to get better, then you have to leave the relationship. If you're unwilling to do so, then you need to redefine your soul's mission and the intention of your essence, including those relationships among the things that you want and choose in your life.

If you truly fear the end of a serious relationship (such as your marriage or a close connection to a family member), take your change slowly, step-by-step, and get lots of guidance. You can start by letting the individual who's involved know what you need and what you're doing. Then ask for input or what he or she needs. If you think counseling as a pair would be beneficial, then seek it out. It's important to have a shared vision as well as your own, and it's okay to explore how changes will impact your relationships.

Making changes that align with your essence is never meant to hurt or upset others, although sometimes it may. Don't jump to conclusions about what people will or won't accept. Give them the chance to be account-able, grow, and make their own choices. If you've been clear about your needs, your offer of support, and your boundaries, and they still refuse to accept you, then you really don't have relationships with these individuals. It's already over.

An essential aspect of knowing your True Self and creating meaning in life *includes* remembering your impact on others and the responsibility of interconnection. Seeking an inspired life isn't an excuse to be cruel, insensitive, or disrespectful toward your commitments and history. If you firmly believe that you need to leave a significant relationship (such as getting a divorce or severing your connection from a family member), it's best to talk with a professional therapist, coach, counselor, or spiritual guide beforehand. You may owe it to the relationship to find a way to grow together.

Coaching and Counseling

Recognizing when you need help from others to end Inspiration Deficit Disorder is not always easy. Asking co-workers, family, or friends for the time, money, or support so that you can see a therapist or coach of some kind can be embarrassing or make you feel like a failure.

Try to put things in perspective: Embarrassment is a Persona reaction because it's all about how you "look" to others, and shame is an old emotion from your Wall of Wounding and is actually a large part of why you got Inspiration Deficit Disorder in the first place. Don't let those emotions stop you! The idea of failure comes from a story that says that everyone should be perfect and never need help . . . but that is a *story* that will eventually ruin your health and your life. While the emotions that block you from asking for help may be real, the rationalizations and excuses are not.

Inspiration Deficit Disorder is an energy crisis by its very nature. You're hooked on the energy of external reactions and behaviors—in other words, your energy is not your own. This is the real reason why you're afraid to break old habits and patterns: the body and mind will lose a source of power they've come to depend on. It feels like the fear of death or total humiliation. It feels impossible. On some level, worrying about losing the energy sources you rely on is a logical and realistic reaction. When you create change and end Inspiration Deficit Disorder, you will struggle with that loss of energy at first.

Very often a significant value to seeking out a therapist, counselor, or coach is that you're able to draw from or "borrow" some of this person's energy so that you're able to take vital steps toward your transformation. These professionals carry the hope, optimism, and positive regard you need to see your way through the dark moments of your inner journey. To break your dependence on an old system, you may require a period where you're supported and know that another perspective is available. A good helper will facilitate your process of identifying your Persona, hooks, and wounds so that you have the freedom to pursue your essence.

The limit to the approach of some therapists is that they seek to help people function "normally" to create peace in the system that they're already a part of. Not all will question whether you are in the right system to begin with! Instead of looking at the soul roots of Inspiration Deficit Disorder, they look at external symptoms, such as depression, confusion, apathy, and anger. If the approach isn't soulful, though, treatment can go on for a long time with little progress. Coaches and therapists with a focus on essence will be interested in helping you express your potential, achieve your dreams, and find a way to live with integrity and joy. Essence-aware helpers will also tend to be more intuitive and heart centered in their work, using a wider tool kit of healing approaches, including visualization, art therapy, mindfulness, or meditation. Their goal should be to become obsolete in your process as soon as possible.

Finding Help

When you seek help, whether it's a spiritual guide, an executive coach, or a psychologist, remember that *you are the customer.* That means you should check out the individual before your first appointment by asking questions and making sure that the two of you would be a good fit. It's okay to ask about people's credentials, how long they've been practicing, and what their approach or philosophy of healing is. The way in which clinicians handle those queries and whether they take the time to give you the answers can tell you a lot.

If you go for one session and "spill your heart out," but by the end you feel like the therapist isn't a good match for you, don't think that you should go back to him or her again just because you started once and don't want to start over. Be willing to start over a few times if you have to! It's best to get the right fit. On the other hand, don't use the "I need to find the perfect therapist/ perfect place/perfect time" excuse to procrastinate. No one is perfect. Trust your heart and use your gut. Pick someone credible and well respected, and get started!

Cost

Good help can sometimes be costly, but it can also be quite reasonable. Many professionals have a "sliding scale" based on what a patient can afford. Help can sometimes also be found in the work or educational program you're involved in. Know that expensive treatments aren't necessarily "good" for you. There are many therapists, life coaches, and soul coaches who can guide you along the process of transformation at reasonable rates. Start by getting clear on what you want out of a therapist/healer and then do some research. Generally, life coaches and soul coaches shouldn't be used as therapists unless they have an appropriate background. If you have deep Wall of Wounding work to do, find a well-trained professional.

How much help you need depends on you, but even a little bit of assistance is beneficial. The American Psychological Association Website is a great place to start looking for someone in your area (**www.apa.org**). It's also a terrific resource to explore and contains a wealth of information. (There's even a glossary of terms that can help you understand common terminology that therapists might use.)

How Often?

Since your helper's role is to keep you on track, be sure to maintain regular contact, at least weekly, even if for only a month or two. Deeper sessions, such as weekend intensives or other programs, can be added as needed after your initial exploration and healing have taken place. Traditional approaches to addiction, trauma, and abuse treatment can be quite long and last years, sometimes at a rate of a session every week or two. Generally, I personally don't recommend long, drawn-out therapy over several years.

If you follow the broad Inspiration Deficit Disorder treatment protocol and really invest in your "inside out" work, therapy for most things shouldn't last more than a few months to half a year. Couples' therapy can take a bit longer. Serious mental-health conditions *should* be treated long-term.

Since I began working in health resorts, however, I've been amazed by the fact that life-changing trans-formations and lasting shifts of profound emotional barriers can happen in a space of just a week or a few days. This is usually a result of the strong intention of the people involved, the focused effort of the providers, and a holistic approach—meaning that all aspects of life are examined in a safe, nurturing environment.

If you really think you need deep emotional help, I certainly recommend consulting a credible psychologist or psychiatrist for advice on how best to address what you're facing. In my opinion, I do *not* feel that the Western psychological and medical approaches are always the best way to go. Too often what is simply a case of Inspiration Deficit Disorder (disconnection from the self) gets diagnosed as a pathology and treated with costly drugs and/or talk sessions that do little to alleviate the situation. I deeply believe in the power of the soul to heal itself in most cases.

Intensives

I've witnessed, experienced, and observed that intensive programs delivering concentrated periods of introspection, healing, and growth are best. Workshops, retreats, and resident programs offer in-depth healing through immersion and community that occasional one-on-one sessions cannot. When my wife, Monica, and I take clients on inspired-living trips to places such as Africa, Mexico, and India, the sheer power of being placed in a foreign setting—removed from daily routines and exposed to new worldviews—can be transformative.

Likewise, the spirit-quest programs I offer, and similar programs run by other organizations, take small groups into wilderness settings for a week or more for a blending of inspired teachings, adventure, relaxation, personal growth, and spiritual practice. I've found that these sorts of intensives have profound and life-altering effects.

Many good examples of such programs are listed on my Website. A fine example of a powerful intensive program (and one that I highly recommend for exploring deep personal issues and fully understanding your Wall and Persona) is called the Hoffman Quadrinity Process. You can learn more about it at **www.hoffmaninstitute.org**.

Life Coaches, Soul Coaches, and Other Guides

Life coaches generally focus on helping clients actualize their goals and plans. They can be a wonderful support during change and ending inspiration deficits.

For many of us, we know what we need to do; we just have a hard time sticking to a plan. Life-coach legend Cheryl Richardson helps with this by connecting people in a special forum called the Life Makeover Group™ Resource Center. You can learn more about this grassroots circle of support at **www.cherylrichardson.com**.

Author and spiritual teacher Denise Linn has created a great Soul Coaching® program; and her graduates are prepared to guide people in the exploration of their essence, spiritual questions, and life calling. To locate practitioners near you, go to **www.soul-coaching.com**. "Spiritual Director" is an older, more traditional term for a spiritual counselor. A helpful association of spiritual directors is Spiritual Directors International, and their Website is **www.sdiworld.org**.

There is a wide range of other healers and guides who can assist your process. Executive coaches, energy psychologists, physicians, fitness professionals, priests, rabbis, gurus, pastors, and other spiritual teachers are all examples of people you may be able to access for support. Be sure they have a background and interest in working as a coach to keep you on task with the change you've envisioned. The key is to match the skill set and training of the individual you pick with what you need him or her to do. Don't ever give up your personal sense of choice and empowerment. Remember that you should feel respect for those who guide you, and if you don't feel safe or respected with your support person, find a new one.

I do also offer people the opportunity to connect with an exceptional team of professionals whom I personally know and trust. You can find their names, contact information, and general information through my Website. (As it has been pointed out, all the resources in this book and more are located on my Website in case you forget or have trouble finding them on your own.)

The Power to Change

"God, grant me the serenity to accept the things I cannot change, the courage to change the things I can, and the wisdom to know the difference."

— REINHOLD NIEBUHR

The classic Serenity Prayer above reminds us of a crucial attitude toward transformation and the embrace of inner peace. One often overlooked element that it points to are the things we cannot change. In the search for inspiration today, a large subculture has emerged that is fixated on the desire, need, and personal capacity to create change. Although very useful, the idea of manifesting and attracting our desires can slip into a kind of denial that life is always full of elements we neither create nor are responsible for.

The final chapter will help you address some of the more "earthly" and material dimensions of inspired living. Sometimes the physical factors in your life—such as your health, where you live, and what you do for a living—are things you can change, but other times you simply can't. You'll eventually understand whether you can modify something in your life or if you simply need to modify your attitude about it.

◎◎◉◎◎

CHAPTER FIFTEEN

Managing Your Physical World: Health, Time, and Space

*"Everybody needs beauty as well as bread, places
to play in and pray in, where Nature may heal and
cheer and give strength to body and soul alike."*

— JOHN MUIR

Inspiration and the Physical World

The energy of your essence is more powerful than you can imagine. In some cases, merely embracing your truth and living with integrity will radically change your well-being and feeling of vitality. Never underestimate the power of your mind and spirit to heal your body. I can almost guarantee that once you commit to ending your Inspiration Deficit Disorder and adopt the principles of living from the inside out, you'll see positive physical changes. I can also assure you that your body impacts your mind and emotions more than you realize, as your mood and attitude are radically shaped by your hormones, neurology, and overall physical condition.

The Physical Costs of Prolonged
Inspiration Deficit Disorder

It's my experience that the longer a person has been living with Inspiration Deficit Disorder, the more likely it is to translate into serious health issues. Many conservative medical professionals would resist admitting the extreme impact of an uninspired life since such a claim is hard to measure or quantify. Yet most people immediately feel the intuitive sense of the possibility. Likewise, most of us see that inspiration deficits are rampant in our medical community today. Burnout, addiction, and suicide among physicians and nurses remain at alarmingly high levels. Having worked closely with physicians and participating as a course contributor in physician education for over ten years, I've seen firsthand how most medical schools as well as the health-care system systematically *create* Inspiration Deficit Disorder in doctors today. Thus, it's with all due respect that I assert the severity of Inspiration Deficit Disorder and accept that some healing professionals will disagree.

If it's not clear to you yet, think of it in this way: if stress is the number one medically agreed-upon factor in creating, aggravating, and contributing to disease, then what creates more stress than a life consumed by bad habits, unmanaged energy, rigid expectations, and a disconnection from the Essential Self? To say that stress is the leading concern in America today is to negate the leading cause of stress: personal imbalance and a lack of authenticity. A lack of self-awareness, inner peace, and self-love will always result in a wide range of unhealthy behaviors, such as poor diet, excessive use of alcohol and coffee, little exercise (or too much), anxiety, busy mind, worry, anger, depression, and fear. Prolonged Inspiration Deficit Disorder leads to the same symptoms as compassion fatigue and post-traumatic stress disorder (PTSD)!

When people come to see me feeling confused and depleted, I immediately ask about their medical history. Most have no reasonable explanation for why they have such low energy or such a hard time sleeping, in addition to poor digestion, agitation, sadness, or any number of other symptoms. It's frustrating and disturbing to feel so sick and not be able to pinpoint the underlying cause. Inspiration Deficit Disorder is the root of more than we realize.

Because there is such a strong connection between a lack of inspiration and high levels of stress and distress, many people with advanced inspiration deficits are on revolving programs of sleeping pills, digestive aids, and blood-pressure and heart medications. Some are on psychoactive meds (like Prozac) to combat their sense of despair. In some cases, these medications will be important and necessary in the long-term because they address a fundamental physiological deficiency. At the same time, all these treatments for a person with Inspiration Deficit Disorder are never going to cure the condition because the inspiration deficit will perpetuate the cycle of disease, allowing the sufferer to continue being frustrated and unaware of the soul psychology at work in his or her imbalance. If unresolved, the condition can eventually become even more severe.

Signs and Symptoms of Advanced
Inspiration Deficit Disorder

A wonderful Website for people with post-traumatic stress disorder is called Helpguide (**www.helpguide .org**). Another helpful site is **www.nimh.nih.gov**, created by the National Institute of Mental Health, which is a branch of the National Institutes of Health. These and other ones like them offer a wide range of information and services for people with this disorder. The overviews they provide on the common symptoms of PTSD are remarkably the very same symptoms that *may* show up in someone with an advanced case of Inspiration Deficit Disorder.

The following list features symptoms that advanced Inspiration Deficit Disorder and PTSD have in common. If you answer *yes* to most of these symptoms, it would be best for you to immediately apply the ten steps to inspired living that were outlined earlier, and seek professional guidance.

- Intrusive, upsetting memories
- Nightmares (either of the traumatic event or of other frightening things)
- Feelings of intense distress
- Intense physical reactions (such as a pounding heart, rapid breathing, nausea, muscle tension, and sweating)
- Avoidance of activities, places, thoughts, or feelings that aggravate your sense of disconnection
- Inability to remember important aspects of how you ended up so far off track

- Loss of interest in activities and life in general
- Feeling detached from others and emotionally numb
- Sense of a limited future (no expectations to live a normal life span, get married, or have a career)
- Difficulty falling or staying asleep
- Irritability or outbursts of anger
- Sleep disorders
- Difficulty concentrating
- Hypervigilance (on constant "red alert")
- Feeling jumpy and easily startled
- Anger and irritability
- Guilt, shame, or self-blame
- Substance abuse
- Eating disorders
- Addictions (sex, gambling, pornography, and so forth)
- Depression and hopelessness
- Suicidal thoughts and feelings
- Feeling alienated and alone
- Feelings of mistrust and betrayal
- Headaches, stomach problems, and chest pain

Again, it should be stressed: *If you have many of these symptoms, your Inspiration Deficit Disorder has already gone too far.* Listening to your heart and following your dreams has gone from an interesting notion to *a critical necessity.* You need to vigorously pursue your health and regain your vitality and passion for life. Be sure you reach out for support.

When Inspiration Deficit Disorder has advanced on your physical health, things like rest, nurturing yourself, light regular exercise, and a healthy diet are essential. Also, if possible, I highly recommend exploring professional programs of detoxification and a prolonged period of rest and recuperation far away from life's demands and stress. Taking a well-formulated supplement designed to assist in your body's healing and repair after trauma, distress, and fatigue can be very helpful.

I also recommend that you explore the Websites of Dr. Andrew Weil (**www.drweil.com**) and Michael's® Naturopathic Programs (**www.michaelshealth.com**), as well as those associated with *Body+Soul* and *Natural Health* magazines. You'll find specialized formulas, helpful customer assistance, and well-researched products. Again, I provide some information about this on my Website, but I also recommend that you research what's available in your area.

Food, Rest, and Movement as Medicine

"When it comes to eating right and exercising, there is no 'I'll start tomorrow.' Tomorrow is disease."

— V.L. ALLINEARE

I won't claim to be an expert on physical health, but having trained in a range of complementary health systems and worked at various teaching hospitals—as well as among some of the nation's most well-respected integrative health practitioners at Canyon Ranch and The University of Arizona's program of integrative medicine—I have a definitive sense of the core elements of this subject. These foundations are widely agreed upon across medical disciplines and healing cultures. My colleagues Stephen Brewer, M.D., and Peggy Holt Wagner, M.S., L.P.C., have written a wonderful and comprehensive book on integrative health and self-care called *The Everest Principle*. Take the time to educate yourself and be sure you always get more than one opinion.

In this section, I will summarize the foundations of a health-promoting and healing lifestyle. Be sure to consult your physician before you take any remedies recommended in this book (or anywhere else) that may complicate or conflict with an existing condition.

Diet

I highly recommend the dietary guidance provided by my friend and colleague Dr. Andrew Weil. In Appendix A of this book, you'll find his very clear diet plan for healthy living, energy, and longevity. Here are some additional points to keep in mind:

- A diet should be personalized to your health goals, age, culture, and body type. Talk to a nutritionist, one of the professionals on my site, or begin your own research.

- Your diet should be high in nutritional content, and you should consume lots of fresh produce (fruits and veggies). Look for foods that are high in fiber and contain the "good fats" like omega-3 and omega-6 fatty acids. Aim for a diet filled with variety and color!

- Your diet should be low in fatty animal protein (sorry—that means eat less red meat and pork), low in foods that are highly processed, and low in additives and preservatives. (If you can't understand half the ingredients in a product or if there are a lot of them, I'd avoid it.)

- Avoid fast food and junk food (yes, that includes most energy drinks and sodas—diet and regular; basically, drinks a gas station would sell).

- Consider a whole-food-based multivitamin (ask someone at a health-food store or in the health section of a store you shop at for help).

- If you absolutely need an energy substitute like coffee in the morning, try an *all-natural* energy supplement or drink formulated by a trusted company. *Most* of the time, what you can buy at your local convenience store will *not* be a healthy choice. There may be some exceptions. Get professional advice before you begin to regularly consume any "energy drinks" to support your health goals. Green and black teas are healthier sources of caffeine.

- Buy organic whenever possible.

- When food shopping, try to buy most of your groceries from the perimeter of the store (fresh breads, produce, fish, and so forth). In other words, avoid the center aisles as much as possible (where everything is in cans, boxes, and plastic bags).

- Consume less caffeine and alcohol! (Much less.)

Rest

More than 10 percent of Americans have been diagnosed with a sleep disorder, and some studies show that nearly 50 percent of Americans report having difficulty sleeping. Poor sleep impacts mood, weight gain, stress, mental clarity, and any existing imbalance. Here are some healthy sleep tips:

- Establish a consistent bedtime routine (for example, stop using your phone and computer 90 minutes before bed, turn the lights down in the house one hour before bed, turn the TV off 30 minutes before bed, have a cup of warm herbal tea, brush your teeth, read for a short time in bed, and then shut off the light).

- Go to bed at the same time every night.

- Get plenty of exercise during the day. The more energy you expend during the day, the sleepier you will feel at bedtime. (Notice whether it's best for you to exercise early in the day or late. Some people are energized by their workouts and cannot sleep for hours after; others find a late-day workout ideal to support a deep sleep.)

- Reduce or eliminate caffeine, stimulants, and alcohol from your diet. All of these can affect sleep.

- Don't eat large meals late at night.

- Practice a relaxation exercise regularly.

- Try breathing techniques, stretching, yoga, visualization, and meditation to help insomnia.

- Take a warm bath before going to bed.

- Get at least 25 minutes of aerobic activity every day.

- Get enough sleep so that you feel rested! Don't cheat on your sleep.

- Don't oversleep to avoid facing your life.

- If you are phasing off a sleep aid or feel you need one, try something natural. I recommend the products by the companies listed at the beginning of this section. I also highly recommend "Restful Night Essentials" created by Dr. Julian Whitaker (**www.drwhitaker.com**). (Remember to always consult your doctor first to make sure that a supplement or medication is safe for you.)

- I also recommend creative visualization. Amazing products that use the best of science and brain-state technology to help you overcome insomnia through music, eyewear, and guided programs can be found at **www.newreality.com**.

Exercise

You should exercise according to your limits and stage of life, but don't use those factors as excuses to avoid improving your physical health. Everyone can do something. Here are more tips:

- Get your heart rate up every day for at least 20 minutes with an aerobic activity such as brisk walking, cycling, rowing, or running. Appendix B provides a physician-recommended guide and sensible advice.

- Strength training is important at all stages of life. It actually becomes more important the older you get. Muscle building aids sleep, digestion, and bone density (among other things). It's best to get personalized strength-training advice, and be careful about what you read in magazines. You should cross-check what you research on your own with a professional at a gym. Leading health centers like Canyon

Ranch recommend strength training at all adult ages, but with caution. Proper form and technique can prevent injury and increase benefits. (See "Fit Specialists" on my Website.)

- If you have concerns about your abilities, consult a doctor.

- Find a trusted source of advice on fitness, and set up a program today. Again, consider consulting some of the magazines and Websites that I've included in this book. There is no replacement for a session with a well-trained professional, though. Fitness professionals are available to you through my Website. Your local YMCA, JCC, or community center may sponsor classes on exercise basics.

Keep Learning

Go to your local gym, recreation center, or health-food store and look for free lectures and classes on fitness, diet, sleep, and health. Be careful about educational seminars that are built around the sale of a product, as the information is often biased and designed to create a focus on the product more than your needs.

Get Organized: Time, Priorities, and Boundaries

Poor time management, overcommitment, and unclear priorities are notorious contributors to Inspiration Deficit Disorder. Even soulful people who have inspired goals can succumb to inspiration deficits when they allow their tasks and responsibilities to overwhelm them. Get yourself a day planner or other type of calendar or on-line system for managing what you have to do, where you have to be, and what your goals are. If you're organized, you'll spend less time worrying and wondering whether you've forgotten something.

I am big fan of an Internet-based program called "Life By Me," which helps you keep track of your tasks, goals, and life priorities in a way that's focused on what is most important to you. It's about being organized *and* inspired. I think just about everyone could use some as-sistance with that. The Website is **www.lifebyme.com**.

Once you begin to log your daily activities and responsibilities, start to evaluate what really matters to you and cut out what isn't necessary. Set priorities and be sure that about 80 percent of what you spend your time doing are things that you can honestly say you see the value in. Activities that you determine are unimportant or feel like pointless obligations should eventually be weeded out!

When you have a clear set of priorities, both in terms of your day-to-day tasks and your big-picture goals, then you have a framework for setting boundaries and saying *no*. Inspiration Deficit Disorder is directly related to how you use and abuse your time. Do you try to cram too much into one day? Do you procrastinate? Are you busy doing what is important to everyone else but you? When you end Inspiration Deficit Disorder, the answer to all these questions should be *no!*

Take time to write, review, and be clear about your *essential vision,* and what you will and won't spend energy on. Set limits. Be clear with other people about what you can and can't do, or how much you will and won't do. Always make time for yourself and your health. A loss of personal time is a common factor in Inspiration Deficit Disorder. Taking even 20 minutes a day or a few 10-minute periods for "me time" throughout the day is key.

If you're able to, set aside a full day once every three months to look at your life path and how you use your time and energy. Write about it, listing what you're currently doing and what you want to be doing, and then compare the two. All great performers, teams, businesses, and high achievers periodically reevaluate the course they're on. If you wait to do it once a year or less, you may find that it's a lot more difficult to make adjustments. More frequent evaluations mean that you won't be able to get as far off track before you can do something about it.

Space and Place

This may be surprising, but your physical environment can be a source of Inspiration Deficit Disorder. If you hate where you live—your home space, work space, or your city—you have a major energy leak. The ideal answer is to: (1) Create an essence-based vision of your life plan, checking with your intuition and your "soul senses" to be clear on what you want and what you need. (2) Do some short-term coaching or therapy to be sure that you're not just reacting to your environment because of old wounds. (3) And then, if absolutely certain, *move!*

Moving isn't something most people can do with ease, mainly due to expense or family ties. I have, however, seen how relocating to a place that feeds someone's essence radically changes that person's life.

For those who don't find their soul's fulfillment in their work, living in a place that has the culture, climate, or lifestyle that inspires them can provide the vital energy they need. For some, it's about saving up enough money to move from an inner-city area to a smaller town, or the reverse. Their work life may remain a secondary source of satisfaction, but their home life and spare time improve. In our recent history, there has been a global mass exodus of people moving from rural settings to urban centers. Looking for new opportunities and a taste of what the big city offers, millions left small cities and towns to find their fortune. Today, however, many people feel trapped in the big cities that they live in and long for a greater connection to nature and a cleaner landscape. A repopulation of smaller centers with a greater emphasis on community and environment could lead a lot of people back to balance.

Make Your Home Your Sanctuary

There are other options to moving. One simple thing is to redecorate or rearrange your home or office in a way that reflects the direction of heart and mind that you seek. The simple trick here is to change what you can, and focus on accepting or finding the best in what you cannot change. You may need to let go of an old story that says the grass is always greener somewhere else. Maybe you can display images, artwork, or tokens from past accomplishments and future goals in your space; or add inspiring photos or soothing colors to your room. Most of these kinds of changes don't need to cost much. It's about surrounding yourself with things that help you feel more like you and staying close to touchstones that will remind you of what is most important.

Your Sacred Space

Another option is to create a sacred space in your home or work environment. This could be a small area, like a room or a corner of a room, where you place a meditation cushion and/or a reading chair. It's essentially an area where you can read, relax, meditate, pray, or do whatever connects you most to your sense of self and spirit. I know people who have created spaces for painting that served as their sacred space, and others have set up designated areas for movement practices such as dance, tai chi, or yoga.

It's also common to have a low bench or table to use as a sort of altar or "special place" to hold important objects and images. An altar is a symbolic display of your inner world and can be elaborate or simple. It's a setting where your Essential Self is showcased—so use objects, images, and books . . . anything that evokes a connection to your essence and feeling of Greater Power.

The Energy of Space

Today a lot of people fantasize about a designer home makeover. They would love to have a decorator come in and pick patterns, colors, and furniture for them so that their living space would look "perfect." This is, in part, a Persona wish. The focus is on image and what others think. Naturally, a good decorator will make your space feel like *you* and reflect your essence, but have you considered placing your decorating focus on *energy* rather than looks—on feeling more than on appearance?

Native cultures have long put great importance on the arrangement of objects and space. It's the essential foundation of a ceremony: objects and movements organized to bring you into connection with a deeper reality. What if you thought of your home as a sacred place, somewhere to recharge? You might want to do some reading on *feng shui* and the placement of objects to maximize the flow of energy and balance in your living space.

Feng shui is an ancient art (and science) that is based on principles similar to those in this book. It suggests that all material objects have a unique energy property, and thus, a unique ability to impact the energy of people, places, and things. You can relate this to times when you've picked up a stone while on a walk that had "good energy" or decided you had to move a piece of art in your house because even though it looked good where it was, "something didn't feel right." You can learn more about this fascinating practice and its practical applications from Ellen Whitehurst's Website and products (**www.ellenwhitehurst.com**). You might also like to check out books by Terah Kathryn Collins.

The Only Thing You Need More of Is Your Essence

"When our eyes see our hands doing the work of our hearts, the circle of Creation is completed inside us, the doors of our souls fly open and love steps forth to heal everything in sight."

— MICHAEL BRIDGE

The world is filled with bright ideas, innovative solutions, and great opportunities. The biggest challenge always lies in finding your own motivation and willingness. In Eastern traditions, there's an old expression about the journey to enlightenment. It's been said that if you don't seek your total liberation of heart and mind with the passion, focus, and conviction of a man with his hair on fire looking for water, then don't bother!

On the other hand, remember that it's okay to stay exactly as you are. There's no need to change, *unless you feel the need*. There's nothing "wrong" unless life doesn't feel right. Listen to your innermost spirit and ask yourself: *Is there more to who I am? Is there more that I have yet to share?*

"More" isn't about what you have or what people think—it's being soulful, mindful, and full hearted. It's about being more *you*. At times, your version of more will be *doing less* and working harder to simply accept yourself as you are. The end of Inspiration Deficit Disorder comes from action, but what that action is will be different for every person. Some people reading this book will say, "Yes! This is the time to slow down," and others will say, "Yes! This is the time to speed up!" The next step is all about what your inner wisdom tells you. It concerns fully embracing who you are and making positive new choices *now*.

Hot and Cold

Do you remember the childhood game "Hot and Cold"? It's when an object is hidden in a room and then someone tries to find it, but the way to do so is by listening to the clues that the "hider" gives. And the hider can *only* use phrases like "getting warmer," "getting colder," or "getting hotter." Try playing it with a child. It's fun! And even more than being amusing, it will teach you a few secrets about life.

First, you're reminded that life won't always deliver a *yes*—that is, your efforts won't automatically be fulfilled. You won't always get "hot" for an answer, but this allows you to realize that being "cold" can be just as helpful. There appears to be no wrong move. Hot or cold, you're still receiving valuable feedback. Even if you don't hear anything but "cold" for a while, that helps you rule out everywhere your goal is *not*. Hearing "hot" isn't necessarily better—it just sounds more successful.

In a similar way, we can be hard on ourselves for relationships, jobs, and diets that fail. Why? Aren't we just ruling out what doesn't work for us? Isn't that also important? It may be that the very process of meeting surprises and disappointments will turn us toward what we need the most. I believe that sometimes life closes doors so that we can be clear about which door we should go through. Too often if we land immediately on something we love, we come to doubt or mistrust it down the road. We wish that we'd explored or experienced more before making our choice.

The critical lesson is that there *is* one wrong move in the game of Hot and Cold—*no move!* Yes, there are certainly times when we need to rest or regroup before taking action, but that in itself is a deliberate "move": the act of self-care. In the game, inaction is just standing there: no feedback, no insight, no learning.

If you're terrified of hearing the word *no* (or *yes*), you might tend to stand still. If your Persona is so hooked on always hearing the world tell you that you're on the right track, you'll never risk being off track. Some people, like those in the stories in this book, are actually afraid of hearing that they're great or deserving of something better.

Take a Step, Pay Attention, and Trust the Process

The bottom line is that the entire universe thrives *not* on the judgments of good and bad, right and wrong, but instead on *feedback* and the openness to integrate new information and make use of it with integrity. Watch nature, as every act in the natural world is a careful response to the feedback of what works and what doesn't. Those who don't honor that law tend to go extinct.

What about you? Is there a step you've been afraid to take? Perhaps one you've been putting off? Take a step and see how it feels. If you're not sure if running is for you, for example, you won't know by reading about it or by looking at pictures of people running. Get out there and do it! See for yourself. If you've never gone to a movie alone, asked someone on a date, attended a yoga class, painted a self-portrait, learned an instrument, volunteered, traveled, stood up to your family, said no to violence, left an unhealthy job or marriage, or refused a drink . . . *try it.* When you take a step, your heart will tell you what is right. In any healthy situation, you can always take a step back if need be.

Don't reverse your decisions out of fear, or always put others first so that you're left feeling depleted or in pain. Living with courage and integrity gives others the chance to do the same. Don't prevent those around you from growing, healing, and learning their own lessons by always doing what makes them comfortable. Maybe the hurt you're afraid of "inflicting" on them isn't really your responsibility. Perhaps it's an opportunity for them to discover more about their own Wall of Wounding, Persona, and the energy hooks that keep them stuck . . .

maybe *you* are one of those energy hooks!

Inspired living replaces fear with soulful discernment. It means to cease reaction and replace it with intention. It puts an end to blind belief and enables you to trust in your Self and the Spirit of Life. Remember the words of the great Buddha who taught a science of inspired living:

> *Believe nothing just because a so-called wise person said it.*
>
> *Believe nothing just because a belief is generally held.*
>
> *Believe nothing because it is said in ancient books.*
>
> *Believe nothing just because it is said to be of divine origin.*
>
> *Believe nothing just because someone else believes it.*
>
> *Believe only what you, yourself, test and judge to be true.*

Honoring Your Essence Honors Others

If you live in absolute integrity, you'll evoke the same in others. If you live in self-doubt and reaction, you'll provoke the same in others. Start today, start now. One small step is all it takes. One step at a time is how you learned to walk, talk, read, drive, and ten million other things. Release your Persona's story about needing to make perfect decisions. Any choice, any action is better than none.

The energy of life responds to clarity, not correctness. If you make a clear wrong choice, you'll quickly sense it. If you stay in confusion and indecision, your inspiration deficit will advance to the point where your body, mind, or heart will be unable to bear the imbalance. You'll find yourself on a crash course for forced change, which isn't the end of the world, but sometimes the damage can be extensive and irreversible. While you have awareness and vision, gather up your courage and begin your transformation today. Always remember that inspired living is a choice.

"People can't live with change if there's not a changeless core inside them. The key to the ability to change is a changeless sense of who you are, what you are about and what you value."

— STEPHEN R. COVEY

◎ ◎ ◉ ◎ ◎

AFTERWORD

Return to The Sacred: The Heart of Spiritual Awakening and Soulful Living

"If the future is to remain open and free, we have to rear individuals who can tolerate the unknown, who will not need the support of completely worked-out systems, whether they be traditional ones from the past or blueprints of the future."

— MARGARET MEAD

One Light, Many Windows

The Cathedral Church of Saint John the Divine in New York City is a remarkable place. This towering gothic cathedral serves not only as a monument to The Sacred, but also as a place that celebrates the human journey and diversity of the world's faith communities. It was there, beneath the soaring arches and timeless architecture, that I was ordained as an interfaith minister.

It was a magnificent ceremony. Priests, rabbis, imams, yogis, monks, and other representatives of leaders of the spiritual community of New York were present. The music was provided by a couple who had dedicated their lives to the cross-cultural study of devotional and religious music; they played various instruments and melodies as familiar and exotic as one could imagine. It was enchanting and deeply moving—each note felt like a plea to the Spirit of Life to draw nearer.

As the ritual unfolded, I found myself searching inward. My training had been rich and challenging, and arriving at the end seemed like a dream. The honor to serve others as a healer and celebrant during life's greatest transitions—such as marriage, birth, death, and loss—evoked tremendous gratitude and a reverence that momentarily overwhelmed me.

Tears streaming down my face, I knew that I was fulfilling a part of myself I couldn't explain, but I had felt its pull for years. Some refer to it as a "calling" or "knowing." Whatever it was, in that moment, I sensed that a piece of my life was falling into place. I was right where I wanted, needed, and felt drawn to be. I realized there would be hard times ahead. I inwardly acknowledged that a lot of the work and future training would be far from easy or comfortable, yet the feeling of completeness I experienced took me beyond my essence and into the embrace of something truly sacred.

In an instant, and beyond thought, I felt a warmth growing in my chest; and my heart felt as if it were glowing, perhaps expanding. Growing as big as the entire room, in my mind's eye my heart became a radiant sphere of light. I breathed love in and out at the very center of that incredible shining life force. It didn't feel like an experience of my own design or influence. Rather, I was nothing more than an instrument, like a flute in the hands of a Greater Power. The Divine breath and holy hands created the music. I only had to surrender.

The next thing I became aware of was the enormous 40-foot-wide circular stained-glass window that watched over our scene. It wasn't a moment of thought, but a feeling, as the light shone through each intricate color and shape of glass. An ocean of soft hues filled the dark cavern of the massive hall. In that instant, it was more than a window, more than a devotion to something holy. It was the Eye of God. I felt the Light of the Divine, streaming in through the brilliant facets of art and glass, high up in the shadows of the seemingly endless ceiling.

That experience was the final unplanned lesson of my program. Beyond word or reason, I *knew* what I was experiencing. It was understanding beyond any doubt that there is a light that shines within and through each and every one of us. The journey toward the essence is only the beginning of inspiration. True inspiration is knowing that you're filled with the Energy of Life, the breath of the Creator Spirit. In whatever way you understand it, that Great and Awesome Mystery holds all power, all potential, and all time. That infinite source and force is the beginning, the end, the context, and the substance of all life. That which we call The Sacred is within you—*it is you.*

Your essence is like a fragile, brilliantly crafted piece of the complex stained-glass window of creation: not better or worse, but equally as awe inspiring as the next. The Wall of Wounding and Persona are the soot and tarnish that cover your magnificence over time. But only you can truly reveal your unique essence. Only you can shine your color, your shape, your design . . . *only you.* The astounding truth is that the Essential Self is what

Creation has asked you to be. The idea of not honoring your authentic self because of guilt, permission, poor timing, or the expectations of others seems absurd when you think of what they're calling you not to be. Not to be amazing? Not to be happy? Not to be a loving, talented heart that embraces and transforms this world?

When you look at it in that way, honoring your essence really isn't about honoring yourself and your own desire for peace and comfort. It's coming home, honoring your origin and beyond. It's a return to The Sacred. Honoring your essence and all that makes you unique is your gift to the world. It's much more than the path to diminish stress, connect with your greatest vitality, and find a fulfilling sense of purpose. When you embark on the journey of revealing your essence, you accept a commitment to be an agent of change in the world, a healer—no matter who you are or what you do.

All this flooded through me beneath that great light, and when my awareness returned to the space and place I was in, I knew I had slipped off for a moment, surpassing my own Wall of Wounding and even my Essential Self. It was the touch of the Eternal, and I will never forget it.

Such experiences don't have to take place in cathedrals or mosques. They can occur anywhere and at any time. I've felt this touch of grace and inspiration in nature, with my wife and son, alone, and with other people. You don't have to go anywhere strange or do anything magical to encounter The Sacred. Just spend the rest of your life asking yourself: *What does it mean to be my truest self? What is my essence? Who have I come here to be?*

The Truth about Inspired Living
and the End of Inspiration Deficit Disorder

"For me, there is no real power without spiritual power.
A power that comes from the core of who you are and
reflects all that you were meant to be. A power that's
connected to the source of things. When you see this
kind of power shining through someone in all its truth
and certainty, it's irresistible, inspiring, elevating."

— OPRAH WINFREY

In the end, your prescription is simple. All the complex philosophy, psychology, medicine, and religion in the world may only keep you from who you were born to be. Life is hard enough; you don't need to make your transformation any more complicated than it has to be. Let it be simple. Do what works, do what you truly love, and be who you are. You don't have to seek enlightenment or the grace of God. You don't have to be the best; or the most successful, rich, or powerful. You don't have to be anything you aren't already. *Be yourself.*

Seek that inexplicable gift that was planted deep within you. It's a seed of light that you need to protect, honor, and nurture. The future, your fate, and all that you worry about will look after itself if you commit to the only thing at hand: unfolding the incredible opportunity to be human—fully, awfully, magically, tragically, and powerfully human. Be powerfully present. Live this moment with clarity, integrity, courage, and compassion. Be present to *what is,* and the rest will fall into place. Trust. The act of inspired living will naturally pull you into the momentum of the essence and beyond.

Show the world who you really are, and you'll feel the vitality and connection you desire. *Be humble, be honest, be you.* It's really that simple.

When you can see the drama of life from the very center of your existence—from the sacred center of it all—you'll realize that inspired living is as simple as loving life unconditionally and letting yourself be loved, just as you are. Accept nothing less. You are more beautiful and important to this world than you will ever know.

The Choice

So we end with a choice. How will you live this moment? Scared or Sacred? Will you choose reaction and desperation or intention and inspiration? The world is waiting for your choice, and there isn't much time. We need you: the planet, the poor, the political, the powerful, the peacemakers. You are the *missing peace.*

Don't look further for answers; *be* the solution. You were born with everything you need to know. Make a promise to stop getting in the way of the blessing that you are. Take a deep breath, remember to have fun, and begin. Find your next step and take it. Know that *you* are needed now more than ever. . . .

> *"We shall not cease from exploration*
> *And the end of all our exploring*
> *Will be to arrive where we started*
> *And know the place for the first time."*

> — T.S. ELIOT

◎◎◉◎◎

APPENDIX A

A Guide to Eating
for an Inspired Life

The following excerpt is reprinted with kind permission from Andrew Weil, M.D., and **www.drweil.com**.

General

- Aim for variety.
- Include as much fresh food as possible.
- Minimize your consumption of processed foods and fast food.
- Eat an abundance of fruits and vegetables.

Caloric Intake

- Most adults need to consume between 2,000 and 3,000 calories a day.
- Women, and smaller and less active people, need fewer calories.
- Men, and bigger and more active people, need more calories.

- If you are eating the appropriate number of calories for your level of activity, your weight should not fluctuate greatly.

- The distribution of calories you take in should be as follows: 40 to 50 percent from carbohydrates, 30 percent from fat, and 20 to 30 percent from protein.

- Try to include carbohydrates, fat, and protein at each meal.

Carbohydrates

- On a 2,000-calorie-a-day diet, adult women should eat about 160 to 200 grams of carbohydrates a day.

- Adult men should eat about 240 to 300 grams of carbohydrates a day.

- The majority of this should be in the form of less-refined, less-processed foods with low glycemic loads.

- Reduce your consumption of foods made with wheat flour and sugar, especially bread and most packaged snack foods (including chips and pretzels).

- Eat more whole grains (not whole-wheat-flour products), beans, winter squashes, and sweet potatoes.

- Cook pasta al dente and eat it in moderation.

- Avoid products made with high-fructose corn syrup.

Fat

- On a 2,000-calorie-a-day diet, 600 calories can come from fat—that is, about 67 grams. This should be in a ratio of 1:2:1 of saturated to monounsaturated to polyunsaturated fat.

- Reduce your intake of saturated fat by eating less butter, cream, cheese (and other full-fat dairy products), unskinned chicken, fatty meats, and products made with coconut and palm kernel oils.

- Use extra-virgin olive oil as a main cooking oil. If you want a neutral-tasting oil, use expeller-pressed, organic canola oil. High-oleic versions of sunflower and safflower oil are acceptable also, preferably non-GMO (genetically modified organism).

- Avoid regular safflower and sunflower oils, corn oil, cottonseed oil, and mixed vegetable oils.

- Strictly avoid margarine, vegetable shortening, and all products listing them as ingredients. Strictly avoid all products made with partially hydrogenated oils of any kind.

- Include in your diet avocados and nuts, especially walnuts, cashews, and almonds and nut butters made from them.

- For omega-3 fatty acids, eat salmon (preferably fresh or frozen wild or canned sockeye), sardines packed in water or olive oil, herring, black cod (sablefish, butterfish), omega-3 fortified eggs, hemp seeds, flaxseeds (preferably freshly ground), and walnuts; or take a fish oil supplement (see "Other Dietary Supplements").

Protein

- On a 2,000-calorie-a-day diet, your daily intake of protein should be between 80 and 120 grams. Eat less protein if you have liver or kidney problems, allergies, or an autoimmune disease.

- Decrease your consumption of animal protein, except for fish and reduced-fat dairy products.

- Eat more vegetable protein, especially from beans in general and soybeans in particular. Become familiar with the range of soy foods available to find ones you like.

Fiber

- Try to eat 40 grams of fiber a day. You can achieve this by increasing your consumption of fruit, especially berries, vegetables (especially beans), and whole grains.

- Ready-made cereals can be good fiber sources, but read labels to make sure they give you at least 4 and preferably 5 grams of bran per one-ounce serving.

Phytonutrients

- To get maximum natural protection against age-related diseases, including cardiovascular disease, cancer, and neurodegenerative disease, as well as against environmental toxicity, eat a variety of fruits, vegetables, and mushrooms.

- Choose fruits and vegetables from all parts of the color spectrum, especially berries, tomatoes, orange and yellow fruits, and dark leafy greens.

- Choose organic produce whenever possible. Learn which conventionally grown crops are most likely to carry pesticide residues (see **www .foodnews.org**) and avoid them.

- Eat cruciferous (cabbage-family) vegetables regularly.

- Include soy foods in your diet.

- Drink tea instead of coffee, especially good-quality white, green, or oolong tea.

- If you drink alcohol, red wine is best.

- Enjoy plain dark chocolate (with a minimum cocoa content of 70 percent) in moderation.

Vitamins and Minerals

- The best way to obtain all of your daily vitamins, minerals, and micronutrients is by eating a diet high in fresh foods with an abundance of fruits and vegetables.

- In addition, supplement your diet with the following antioxidant cocktail:

  —Vitamin C, 200 milligrams a day

  —Vitamin E, 400 IU of natural mixed tocopherols (d-alpha-tocopherol with other tocopherols, or, better, a minimum of 80 milligrams of natural mixed tocopherols and tocotrienols)

  —Selenium, 200 micrograms of an organic (yeast-bound) form

  —Mixed carotenoids, 10,000 to 15,000 IU daily

- In addition, take daily multivitamin-multimineral supplements that provide at least 400 micrograms of folic acid and at least 1,000 IU of vitamin D. They should contain no iron and no preformed vitamin A (retinol).

- Take supplemental calcium, preferably as calcium citrate. Women need 1,200 to 1,500 milligrams a day, depending on their dietary intake of this mineral; men should get no more than 1,200 milligrams of calcium a day from all sources.

Other Dietary Supplements

- If you are not eating oily fish at least twice a week, take supplemental fish oil, in capsule or liquid form, 1 to 2 grams a day. Look for molecularly distilled products certified to be free of heavy metals and other contaminants.

- Talk to your doctor about going on low-dose aspirin therapy, one or two baby aspirins (81 or 162 milligrams) a day.

- If you are not regularly eating ginger and turmeric, consider taking these in supplemental form.

- Add Co-Q-10 to your daily regimen: 60 to 100 milligrams of a softgel form taken with your largest meal.

- If you are prone to metabolic syndrome, take alpha-lipoic acid, 100 to 400 milligrams a day.

Water

- Try to drink 6 to 8 glasses of pure water a day or drinks that are mostly water (tea, very diluted fruit juice, sparkling water with lemon).

- Use bottled water or get a home water purifier if your tap water tastes of chlorine or other contaminants or if you live in an area where the water is known or suspected to be contaminated.

ⓞⓞ◉ⓞⓞ

APPENDIX B

Natural Energy:
Basic Exercise Advice
with an Aerobic Focus

Aerobic exercises are activities that get your heart working, such as brisk walking, swimming, or cycling. The following information and good advice is courtesy of Andrew Weil, M.D., and **www.drweil.com**.

1. Any aerobic exercise is better than no aerobic exercise. I would be happy to see you doing even a few minutes of it on a regular basis, but if you want to experience all the benefits, try to do some continuous aerobic activity for thirty minutes a day, on average, five days a week.

2. Remember to work up to this level gradually and at your own pace, especially if you have not been exercising.

3. Remember also that I am recommending an *average* amount of activity over time. It is not the end of the world if you miss a day or two here and there. You can make it up later.

Feeling bad about missing exercise probably does you more harm than missing it.

4. In addition to these workouts, find other ways to increase your daily activity, such as using stairs more often, parking farther from your destinations to walk more, and doing more physical work yourself instead of delegating it to others.

5. If you exercise with others, try not to do so competitively. Competitive thoughts negate some of the benefits of exercise, especially on your cardiovascular and immune systems and emotions. If you cannot avoid competitive thinking, exercise by yourself.

6. Competitive sports like racquetball, handball, and tennis are not substitutes for aerobic activities such as walking, running, and cycling. In competitive sports, aerobic work is of a stop-and-go nature rather than continuous. It is regular, continuous effort that tones your cardiovascular system best.

7. Always warm up before you get into the full swing of aerobic activity. The best warmup is a slowed-down version of the activity you are about to perform. For example, walk, run, or cycle in slow motion. You will see many people stretching as a warmup, but this does not prepare muscles for aerobic exercise as well as slow movement does.

8. Give yourself a few minutes of cool down at the end of the activity. Repeat the same movements in slow motion.

9. If you have never exercised, get a medical checkup before you start an exercise program. If you have a history of heart trouble or high blood pressure or a strong family history of such problems, a cardiac stress test may be in order.

10. Pay attention to your body! Discontinue or change your specific exercise if you develop unusual aches or pains.

11. Stop exercising immediately if you develop dizziness, lightheadedness, chest pains, or difficulty in breathing. Get a medical checkup promptly.

12. Your heart rate and breathing should return to normal within five to ten minutes after the end of aerobic exercise. If they do not, get a medical checkup.

13. Do not exercise if you are sick. Wait until you feel better, then resume gradually. Don't worry about losing fitness; it will come back quickly enough. Strenuous exercise at the onset of illness can cause you to be sicker longer.

◎◎◉◎◎

INSPIRED-LIVING RESOURCES

As mentioned throughout this book, I've tried to make all the details, links, and resources included here available on my Website: **www.jonathanellerby.com**.

Members of my site can also receive a free audio program, videos, articles, and other tools that complement the material in this book. To support you on your journey, I've developed a simple, inexpensive, and effective workbook you can use to create and monitor personalized plans based on this book and its recommendations. You can use the Inspired Life Workbook to create the plans, steps, and visions you need to actualize the transformation you envision.

If you have a specific interest in spirituality and spiritual practices in your inspired life, I recommend that you consider two helpful resources I've created: *Return to The Sacred: Pathways to Spiritual Awakening* (a Hay House book) and *Your Spiritual Personality: Finding the Path That's Right for You* (an 8-CD audio-learning course, published by Sounds True).

❀❀❀❀❀

ACKNOWLEDGMENTS

As ever, there are so, so many people to thank for any creation. And, as ever, I want to begin by thanking each and every unnamed soul who directly or indirectly contributed to this book and the material in it.

First, I want to thank all the people who have come to me for help, healing, coaching, and ceremony—especially those who anonymously appear in this book. Your trust and willingness have meant the world to me, and you've taught me more than any instructor or textbook could. It has been my honor to serve you, and I truly feel that I have received more than I have given. So it's with humility that I say that this is really your book. I'm just the messenger.

I can go no further without thanking my wife, my hero and an amazing living expression of the lessons in this book. For your courage to transform and find your truth, I am forever in awe and in love! Thank you for your support and tolerance of all the demands that go along with my books and career. To my son, Narayan—there are no words to tell you what a blessing you are to me. My guru-ji, you are Living Spirit and Pure Joy. You remain my greatest spiritual practice and divine teacher. Love is too small a word for what I feel for you.

To my mom who gave me the wisdom and encouragement at a young age to pay attention to my Essential Self; also for her astonishing strength of spirit and boundless love. To my dad, who understood little about my pursuits but always made my journey possible and knew enough to love me unconditionally. For the love and living examples of inspired living, I thank my sister, Shauna; my brother, Lawrence; my sister-in-law, Brenda; and my niece, Jess. You are all more a part of my life than you know.

To my spiritual dad, Gene, for the deep lessons in healing and how to help. To *all* of my relations in Wase Wakpa and the Vermillion area for being a part of my journey. To Mark Samuel for teaching me so much about how to facilitate groups and individuals in a way that is simple, clear, and always powerful. To all my mentors and teachers of counseling, chaplaincy, healing, and coaching—thank you.

To the amazing Ned Leavitt for agency, song, and friendship.

To the incredible gang at Hay House, for your amazing work in the world and for supporting my work. Especially to Reid Tracy, who continues to include me in his kindness and clear vision. To Stacey Smith, for your grace and connection. Much gratitude to Lisa Mitchell for your wise mind and open heart; Charles McStravick for your gifted hands and brilliant eye. There are many others there to thank and mention: Jill Kramer, Carina Sammartino, Jacqui Clark, Jeannie Liberati, Nancy Levin, John Thompson, and on and on! Thank you all.

To all the wonderful Wasabi crew, especially Michelle and Drew, for your faith in me and your sincere heart. To Jill Mangino, for your generosity and friendship. And for all those who supported the vision behind this book, believed in me, and helped me learn about how to present myself to the public world: Ana Weber,

Mary Jo Rose, Steven Goldstein, Margaret Roach, Terri Trespicio, Holly Rossi, Jenny Love, Chris Shaw, Jamie Afifi, Arielle Ford, Maggie Gallant, Kim Fanti, the incredible Ellen Whitehurst, Pete Dupuis, Sharon Kieffer, Hilary Crnkovich, and Scott and the team at Token Rock. For all the Web support and personal assistance, I thank "Zen John" and Rachel. To Larry and Max for your invaluable help, friendship, and brilliant care of my correspondence. To all my wonderful readers of my first draft, not limited to but including Erica, Lisa, and amazing Nikki (you inspire me!).

To my magnificent circle of support at Canyon Ranch, especially to the Executive team and to all those at Health and Healing who make my comings and goings possible (Pam, you know that means especially you!). As always, to Jerry and Mel for your special attention and support. Also to those of you who shine a light on my work—Carrie, Jim, Shirley, Sarah, and Ramona.

Finally, to my dear friends who have supported my work with encouragement—there are too many to list. A few that need mention because in one way or another you gave me a boost while I wrote this: Mark Naseck, Majeed, Tamara, Peter Beach (I still have to thank you!), James Pappas (yes, you too), Sophie Chiche, Joan Borysenko and Gorden Deveirin, Gregg Braden, Christiane Northrup, Ken Blanchard, John Dore, Andrew Weil, and Oriah and Larry Dossey (your friendship still encourages me). Special thanks to Sandy Muss for your deep kindness and support. So much gratitude to Lisa "Two Hawks" for your support and sacred writing space!

Lisa Redstone, you deserve a category of your own! How can I thank you for your absolute support in every way? You are a gift to me and a blessing to my family and all whom you work with. You've contributed to this book and my work in astounding ways.

Another extraordinary individual who deserves my deepest graditude and love is the wonderful Karen Lytle. Thank you for all you have shared, your support, and your belief in my work.

For all those who have read my work or attended my workshops and lectures, thank you for your support, kind works, and encouragement.

For anyone I have forgotten, forgive me, for I thank you, too.

Finally, to the only *One* that really exists, the One Spirit and Original Source, I radiate gratitude for life and all that I am! May I always serve in a spirit of love and connection.

⊚ ⊚ ◉ ⊚ ⊚

ABOUT THE AUTHOR

Jonathan Ellerby, Ph.D., is an important guide to inspired living in today's hectic world, bridging cultures and professional disciplines to help people find what works. Featured as an expert in film, print, television, and radio, Jonathan is the author of *Return to The Sacred: Pathways to Spiritual Awakening* and the Spiritual Program Director for the internationally acclaimed Canyon Ranch Health Resorts in Tucson, Arizona. With a Ph.D. in comparative religion and over 20 years of experience in the fields of holistic healing, counseling, integrative medicine, and corporate consulting, Jonathan makes spirituality simple. Drawing from his travels around the world and experiences with healers from more than 40 cultural traditions, he focuses on what works to bring balance and inspiration to everyday life.

Website: **www.jonathanellerby.com**

⊚ ⊚ ◉ ⊚ ⊚

NOTES

NOTES

NOTES

NOTES

NOTES

NOTES

NOTES

Hay House Titles of Related Interest

YOU CAN HEAL YOUR LIFE, the movie,
starring Louise L. Hay & Friends (available as a 1-DVD
program and an expanded 2-DVD set) Watch the trailer at:
www.LouiseHayMovie.com

THE SHIFT, the movie, starring Dr. Wayne W. Dyer
(available as a 1-DVD program and an expanded 2-DVD set)
Watch the trailer at: **www.DyerMovie.com**

◉ ◉ ◉

*EXCUSES BEGONE! How to Change Lifelong, Self-Defeating
Thinking Habits,* by Dr. Wayne W. Dyer

*HEALING YOUR FAMILY HISTORY: 5 Steps to Break Free of
Destructive Patterns,* by Rebecca Linder Hintze

*INSPIRED DESTINY: Living a Fulfilling and Purposeful
Life,* by Dr. John F. Demartini

*IT'S NOT THE END OF THE WORLD: Developing Resilience
in Times of Change,* by Joan Borysenko, Ph.D.

*MODERN-DAY MIRACLES: Miraculous Moments and
Extraordinary Stories from People All Over the World
Whose Lives Have Been Touched by Louise L. Hay,*
by Louise L. Hay & Friends

*THIS IS THE MOMENT! How One Man's Yearlong Journey
Captured the Power of Extraordinary Gratitude,*
by Walter Green

*UNLOCK THE SECRET MESSAGES OF YOUR BODY!
A 28-Day Jump-Start Program for Radiant Health
and Glorious Vitality,* by Denise Linn

All of the above are available at your local bookstore,
or may be ordered by visiting:

Hay House USA: **www.hayhouse.com**®
Hay House Australia: **www.hayhouse.com.au**
Hay House UK: **www.hayhouse.co.uk**
Hay House South Africa: **www.hayhouse.co.za**
Hay House India: **www.hayhouse.co.in**

We hope you enjoyed this Hay House book. If you'd like to receive our online catalog featuring additional information on Hay House books and products, or if you'd like to find out more about the Hay Foundation, please contact:

Hay House, Inc., P.O. Box 5100, Carlsbad, CA 92018-5100
(760) 431-7695 or (800) 654-5126
(760) 431-6948 (fax) or (800) 650-5115 (fax)
www.hayhouse.com® • **www.hayfoundation.org**

◦ ⊙ ◎

Published and distributed in Australia by: Hay House Australia Pty. Ltd., 18/36 Ralph St., Alexandria NSW 2015 • *Phone:* 612-9669-4299 *Fax:* 612-9669-4144 • www.hayhouse.com.au

Published and distributed in the United Kingdom by: Hay House UK, Ltd., 292B Kensal Rd., London W10 5BE • *Phone:* 44-20-8962-1230 • *Fax:* 44-20-8962-1239 • www.hayhouse.co.uk

Published and distributed in the Republic of South Africa by: Hay House SA (Pty), Ltd., P.O. Box 990, Witkoppen 2068 • *Phone/Fax:* 27-11-467-8904 • info@hayhouse.co.za • www.hayhouse.co.za

Published in India by: Hay House Publishers India, Muskaan Complex, Plot No. 3, B-2, Vasant Kunj, New Delhi 110 070 • *Phone:* 91-11-4176-1620 • *Fax:* 91-11-4176-1630 • www.hayhouse.co.in

Distributed in Canada by: Raincoast, 9050 Shaughnessy St., Vancouver, B.C. V6P 6E5 • *Phone:* (604) 323-7100 *Fax:* (604) 323-2600 • www.raincoast.com

◦ ⊙ ◎

Take Your Soul on a Vacation

Visit **www.HealYourLife.com®** to regroup, recharge, and reconnect with your own magnificence. Featuring blogs, mind-body-spirit news, and life-changing wisdom from Louise Hay and friends.

Visit **www.HealYourLife.com** today!

HEAL YOUR LIFE ♥

Take Your Soul on a Vacation

Get your daily dose of inspiration today at **www.HealYourLife.com®**. Brimming with all of the necessary elements to ease your mind and educate your soul, this Website will become the foundation from which you'll start each day. This essential site delivers the latest in mind, body, and spirit news and real-time content from your favorite Hay House authors.

Make It Your Home Page Today!

www.HealYourLife.com®